The Story of Charles Dickens

Charles Dickens, at 56

THE STORY OF

Charles Dickens

by Eleanor Graham

*Illustrated with plates
from the original editions of his works
and with additional drawings
by Norman Meredith*

Abelard-Schuman, New York

Printed and bound in the
United States of America

FOR THEO

CONTENTS

CONTENTS

ILLUSTRATIONS

~~~~~~~~~~~~~~~~~~~~~~~~~~~~~~~~~~

CHAPTER I

Early Days

CHARLES DICKENS WAS NOT BORN WITH A SILVER SPOON IN
his mouth. His father and mother were careless
parents, too much occupied with their own lives to
spare much thought for their home or the bringing up
of their children. Charles remembered being seized by
the hair and scrubbed from neck to scalp to make him
presentable for church, but did not remember being
trained to keep himself clean and tidy, nor to speak
the truth or to be brave or in earnest over anything.

In his books he drew many pictures of wretched
homes such as he knew very well from his own experience. He knew how it felt to be sent out to the
pawnbroker with the spoons they commonly used at
table in order to get a little ready money, or to go
shamefacedly into little shops for an ounce or two of
tea and a scrap of cheese, asking credit which the shop-
keepers were unwilling to give. He saw his parents
practicing all sorts of tricks to avoid paying money
they owed. Yet they were not "poor." John Dickens
was a clerk in the Civil Service and was earning two
hundred pounds a year ($1000) when he married;
and it was three hundred and fifty by the time Charles
was eight. Those sums would be worth at least three
times as much today.

In the early days of the Dickens' marriage, when

they were young and handsome and happy-go-lucky, it did not seem to matter whether ends met or not. Someone always helped them out. John's mother, though she was a widow keeping herself as house-keeper in a big house, gave him money over and over again, but she was growing old and John was not her only son. His wife's family, the Barrows, were in better circumstances and they helped too until it began to appear that they were doing no good, but simply encouraging bad ways. Shops gave credit easily then so Mr. and Mrs. Dickens spent carelessly, and debts soon mounted. It was unpleasant when they found themselves pressed to pay, but they only learned from that to make up excuses. Charles drew his parents' pictures in several of his books when he grew up. Anyone who reads *David Copperfield* sees one side of John Dickens in Mr. Micawber. In *Little Dorrit* there is another in "the father of the Marshalsea." In the same way he drew his mother as Mrs. Micawber and also as Mrs. Nickleby.

Charles was born at Portsmouth in south England on February 7, 1812. His sister Fanny was then fifteen months old. The family was living in a nice little house (now kept as a Dickens Museum), but they moved when he was still very young. He remembered little of it but the garden in front, watching soldiers on parade, and learning to run between the arms of his mother and those of a kneeling servant.

Navy Pay Office clerks were liable to be sent to any of His Majesty's Dockyards (what we would call ports), and that was how the Dickens' came to be in Portsmouth, but when Charles was two they were moved to London. Before they could go, they had to settle their debts. It looks as though the furniture was

sold to pay them, for in London they lived in a furnished apartment.

Another son and daughter were born during this
time. The son died in a few months, but the girl,
Letitia, was healthy. In 1817 Mr. Dickens was moved
again, this time to Chatham, and the happiest period
of Charles' childhood began.

Mrs. Dickens had a widowed sister, who knew
Chatham and suggested going with them, to keep
house and share expenses. The idea was welcomed as
Mrs. Dickens was not practical and hardly knew what
to do with three children under seven.

Their new house was in Ordnance Terrace, one of
a short row, well built, with basement kitchen, large
cellars and, out at the back, a bakery with big bread
ovens. Charles slept in the front attic, which looked
over the town to where the river Medway ran in great
snaky loops towards the Estuary. From its windows
he could see the tall masts of East Indiamen lying at
anchor there, some battered by gales and heavy seas
during their long voyages round the Horn, others waiting, trim and shipshape, to set out again for distant
ports. By leaning out of the window, he could see
the masts and chimneys of the Navy Dockyard and
the green hillsides, cornfields and orchards behind it.
Soldiers in scarlet coats and pipe-clayed belts drilled
between the Yard and the Terrace, and the echo and
snap of the orders must often have floated up to him
there.

From the Terrace the ground ran down to the old
town and the river beyond. Between the High Street
and the water was the usual huddle of chandlers'
shops and marine stores, dark and cavernous for the
most part, a couple of steps lower than the doorways,

Ordnance Terrace, Chatham
The Dickens' lived in the second house from the left

stocked with barrels and kegs, coils of rope, ships' lanterns and other gear, all smelling of tar and oil. What with these and the Dockyard, with ships always coming and going, with sailors and soldiers and Dockyard workers, Chatham was a grand place for a boy to live in. Even a day in bed need not be dull—and Charles was often in bed with a stitch in his side, bad enough to keep him awake at night, and lasting for days at a time.

His father or Mary Weller, one of the servants— they had three—often came to sit with him then and told him stories. Mr. Dickens' tales were not very exciting in themselves. They were anecdotes of people he had known or things he had heard about, but the way he told them, throwing back his shoulders and swaying his great head, playing with his eye glasses or the bunch of keys which hung from his watch-chain, made them as good as a play to Charles. Mary Weller's stories were different, tales to make your flesh creep, about ghosts, murders and highwaymen, or of births and deathbeds. Mary belonged to Chatham and knew everyone in the little streets. When Charles was well, and she could slip out at night, she often took him with her—"for protection" he thought. Many a time he waited for her in tiny cottage kitchens, imagining all kinds of lurid scenes from the muffled sounds which reached him from rooms above.

The family next door in Ordnance Terrace was called Stroughill. There were a boy, George, and a girl, Lucy, about Charles' and Fanny's ages. They were soon great friends, running in and out of each other's houses and sharing games and treats. George had a magic lantern which he brought into the Dickens' house sometimes, and they showed their slides against a sheet hung up in the kitchen. There would be songs and recitations, too, by Charles and Fanny. Mary Weller lived to see Charles famous and recalled then how he used to dash upstairs when everything was ready, shouting to the grown-ups, "Come and see the fun!" and she described him reciting with "such gestures! such attitudes!" This amused his father, too, so that sometimes he took young Charles along to entertain his friends at the Mitre, where they used to set him up on a table, guffawing at his antics as they drank their wine. Mr. Dickens was partial to a glass of wine.

By the time Charles came to Chatham he had learned his ABC's more or less from his mother. He could pick them out on newspaper headlines or street notices, but was a long way from reading a book, and they had few books anyway. Mr. Dickens, however, subscribed for a set which had been advertised as forming the nucleus of every gentleman's library, and the score or so of volumes were delivered in a huge, heavy parcel. It had been set down inside the front door and lay about there for weeks unopened. Then, after stumbling over it once too often, Mrs. Dickens called the servants and told them angrily to take it upstairs to the attic out of the way. There Charles found it one day when he was laid up with one of his spasms. He saw the books through a hole someone had torn in the wrappings, pulled one out and carried it back to bed. After he had laboriously spelled out a page or two he began to see the shape of a story, and soon felt it taking hold of him. He finished learning to read on those books and then, with growing excitement, discovered that there was *pleasure* in reading.

He found, in that parcel of books, *Robinson Crusoe,*

*Gulliver's Travels, The Arabian Nights, Tales of the
Genii, Don Quixote, Gil Blas, The Vicar of Wakefield,
Tom Jones, Peregrine Pickle, Roderick Random, Humphrey Clinker*—exactly those he mentioned later in
David Copperfield when (in Chapter IV) he said,
"From that blessed little room they came out, a glorious host, to keep me company. I consoled myself
under my small troubles by impersonating my favorite characters in them. I have been Tom Jones (a
child's Tom Jones, a harmless creature) for a week
together. I have sustained my own idea of Roderick
Random for a month at a stretch. I had a greedy
relish for a few volumes of Voyages and Travels—I
forget what now—and for days and days have gone
about my region of our house, armed with the center
piece of an old set of boot-trees—the perfect realiza-
tion of Captain Somebody of the Royal British Navy,
in danger of being beset by savages, and resolved to
sell his life at a great price. . . . Every barn in the
neighborhood, every stone in the church, and every
foot of the churchyard, had some association of its
own in my mind connected with these books." And,
as a man, looking back at those times, Dickens remembered himself sitting on his bed, "reading as if
for life."

"Aye, he was a terrible boy to read," Mary Weller
agreed.

Nothing could distract him from a book, not even
the shouts of the other children at play. He had that
sort of concentration all his life. But he turned the
stories into games which they all played—Ali Baba and
the forty thieves, Crusoe and Man Friday, Gil Blas
in the robbers' cave—and even Mary and her young

man from the Dockyard listened to them and asked for more.

Sometimes, as a treat, Mr. Dickens took his son with him when he went to work, and Charles felt proud and important as they passed the sentry at the gates. His father had to go indoors and spend his morning on a high stool, but Charles was free to go where he liked so long as he did not get in anyone's way. He sped past the stores of cannon on the gun-wharf. He watched pile-driving and sluice-making, blacksmiths and carpenters. He inspected the sailyards, ropemakers' alleys and the masthouse. He watched the cranes at work, delighted when he caught the giant arm swinging some huge, whole tree trunk into the seasoning vats, or from vat to sawmills; and, being that kind of a person, he noticed the men as well as what they did. He noticed the blacksmiths singing at their anvils, as he made Joe Gargery sing in *Great Expectations*. It was there, too, that he first saw those "ugly mastless boats with roofs like a Noah's Ark," known as "the hulks," in which convicts, sentenced to transportation to Botany Bay or some other of the penal settlements, awaited shipment. He saw gangs brought ashore from them, in chains, to work in the Yard. It was there he first heard the story of the carpenter and the devil who claimed him with the words, "A lemon has pips, a Yard has ships, and I'll have Chips."

He was seeing Chatham at the tail end of the sailing-ship days, for steamers were already running between Dover and Calais, but for him every movement of the tall ships was of immense interest. He marked their coming and going and learned all about the ceremonies which attended their arrival and departure.

Mr. Dickens was sent to Sheerness from time to time on the Pay Office's yacht, the *Chatham*, built when Cromwell was Protector of England. This sometimes meant a treat for Charles and Fanny, and possibly for the Stroughills, too. As their boat drew away, Charles searched swiftly for the familiar landmarks before they merged together under the smoke of the Yard's many chimneys. And when the clank of the hammers, the purr of the sawmills, and the thousand and one noises of the busy place fell behind them, there were the river craft to watch, the puffing little steam tugs, heavy old colliers, barks and schooners, yachts and sailing boats.

These were great occasions, provided by his father, so it is not surprising that Charles admired him deeply and tried to copy the jaunty walk and the curving lips which brought forth those flourishes of speech in which Mr. Dickens gloried, and which echo through the pages of *Pickwick, David Copperfield,* and others of Dickens' stories. At home, thanks to his aunt's good management, there were order and comfort and plenty. No wonder Charles took it for granted that he had a place in the world, and began to dream of becoming Somebody one day, of being a Gentleman, which to him meant being well educated and a man of culture and dignity.

On pleasant Sunday mornings he and his father used to take a walk into the country, ending up somewhere for a glass of wine. One of their favorite haunts was Gadshill, reached by way of Rochester, past those timbered houses in which, in the world of Charles' imagination, Uncle Pumblechook and Mr. Sapsea were to make their homes. They crossed the old bridge on which, he was told, men worked for a penny a day in 1307 when it was built. On the other side, their path lay through meadows and orchards up to the low hill on which stood the John Falstaff Inn. The place cast a spell on Charles, and even his father felt something, and liked to pause outside the whitewashed walls, to strike an attitude and declaim Shakespeare's lines: "But my lads, my lads, tomorrow morning by four o'clock early at Gadshill. There are pilgrims going to Canterbury with rich offerings, and traders riding to London with fat purses. I have vizards [masks] for you all. You have horses for yourselves."

It was there, on Gadshill, that Falstaff went out to rob the travelers and ran away. The Inn dates from about that time. It stands on the old Dover Road, which was the pilgrims' road to Canterbury and the Roman road before that.

Just across from the Inn there was a comfortable red brick house, a gentleman's residence, large but plain, about forty years old, with a semicircular drive between its two white gates. Staring at it, Charles fell into a day dream. It was the sort of house he wanted when he grew up. It spelled for him the kind of life he wanted to lead. Confidingly, he inquired whether his father thought it possible that he really might live there one day. John Dickens, immensely tickled, assured him glibly that there was no reason why not, if he persevered and worked hard; and his words sounded like a promise to young Charles.

Many years after that house did become his home. He persevered as his father had said he should, and he endured such hardships and discouragement that all thought of it had entirely gone out of his head when an opportunity to buy it came his way by the merest chance. He had by then had other houses as good or better than Gadshill Place, but none was ever so dear to him nor suited him so well as the one whose shadow had fallen so pleasantly across his path in those early days.

~~~~~~

CHAPTER II

The Outlook Darkens

ALL TOO SOON THE PATTERN OF LIFE IN ORDNANCE Terrace was broken by the news that Aunt Mary intended to marry again. She had met a surgeon called Lamert at the Chatham Military Hospital. He was comfortably off, a widower with one son, James, who was waiting for a commission in the Army. James had time on his hands and spent it on amateur theatricals in his father's roomy quarters at the hospital. He had already made friends with Charles, patronizing him delightfully from the lordly heights of his seventeen years. He had heard the reciting, too, and set about showing him how words should be spoken. He talked to him about plays and acting, took him to the theater at Chatham and once up to London, to the Pantomime at Drury Lane to see Grimaldi, the great clown whose fame has never died.

That was a day to remember! It was in January and so cold that Charles' toes in his new boots were numb even before the stage coach had crossed Rochester Bridge. But once in the theater, the cold was forgotten and, when the curtain went up, his eyes never left the stage. He laughed uproariously and clapped until his palms smarted. He hardly spoke to James until they were on their way home again. Then he wanted to know all kinds of things. Why was Grimaldi's face so white? Was he born so? Did clowns remain clowns all their lives? Did he really eat the strings of sausages? Did anyone ever object to the tricks he played on them? Did they think he had really stolen their property and send for the police?

Charles was not quite eight that day, but eighteen years later, when he edited Grimaldi's *Memoirs*, he was able to use his own vivid recollections of the clown's act.

Meanwhile the preparations for his aunt's wedding were going ahead. Dr. Lamert decided to leave the hospital and settle in Ireland, so James was to stay with the Dickens' until he got his commission. The money for his keep was no doubt intended to make up for the loss of Aunt Mary's contribution to household expenses.

No sooner had the Lamerts gone, than bills began to pour in, not all of them strictly incurred for the wedding. The cellars at Ordnance Terrace with their wine vaults and cradles had proved too great a temptation to Mr. Dickens. Now the tradesmen wanted their money and, as usual, Mr. Dickens had none to give them. He passed the hat around among relatives and friends without much success, so he decided to cut his expenses and move to a cheaper house. He sold some of his furniture and dismissed the servants. Mary Weller begged to stay, as she hoped to get married soon and did not want to find another place for so short a time; so, for less wages, she stayed.

From their pleasant home on the heights, they now moved into a small box of a place on the low ground near the Dockyard, a plain little workman's house without elegancies of any kind. It stood beside a Baptist chapel, which is now a shabby old warehouse, though the shape of the chapel is still clear. The min-

ister there had a son who wanted to start a school and
began by teaching his own brothers and sisters.
The Dickens' children joined them, and soon the
Stroughills as well. The move made little difference to
the children's friendship. They had further to go now,
and the Stroughills had the advantage of running
downhill to Charles' house, while he and Fanny had to
climb up to theirs.

Their new teacher, William Giles, saw great promise in Charles' eagerness to learn, his bright intelligence, high spirits and his tremendous zest for every
kind of experience. Giles understood ambition, knew
how to teach, and taught his pupils well. It was he
who gave Charles the nickname of "The Inimitable,"
which was heard in moments of elation all through
Dickens' famous career. Giles soon had a successful
academy which justified his taking a house for it
with a playground for the boys. They became known
locally as "Giles Cats"—but that meant little in a town
where others had "Troy Town Rats," "Baker's Bull-
dogs" and "New Town Scrubbers" yelled after them.

With Giles spurring him on, lending him books and
making him think about them, Charles probably had
his first glimmering of an idea of a career. He may have
dreamed of achieving it by way of a university,
though his circumstances then would have made that
difficult. His hopes ran so high, he hardly noticed
what was happening at home. He admired his father
too much to doubt him or to question his wisdom, and
thanks to Mary Weller, the home was still pretty well
run. Yet Charles was too observant to have missed altogether the signs of trouble brewing, of the increasing
burden of debt and the slight change in the attitude of
storekeepers.

About a year after they had moved to St. Mary's
Terrace, John Dickens learned that he was to be trans-
ferred to London immediately. He knew that the fat
would be in the fire with a vengeance. The news was
bound to get out, and he would be faced with bills he
could not possibly pay. Putting on his most "Micaw-
berish" face, he tried to borrow wherever he thought he
had the slightest chance of success. He sold the rest
of his furniture, and offered his creditors a little here
and a little there, with solemn assurances of payment
in full the moment his "expectations" were realized.
Mary Weller bought the parlor chairs (and they can
still be seen in the Museum in Rochester).

The news of this move shocked Charles into real-
izing something of their circumstances, and he begged
to be left with Mr. Giles. The request must have
surprised his parents for he was an affectionate son.
They were wounded by it, but in the end they let him
stay.

Before they left, Mrs. Dickens paid a visit to the
workhouse (in which, later on, Charles was to put
Oliver Twist), to select an orphan girl to be her
servant. In later years, Charles wrote of her as "The
Marchioness" in *The Old Curiosity Shop*, and as "the
Orfling" in *David Copperfield*.

Charles stayed at Chatham for a few more months,
went to school and rambled about the country he
loved, and was to love so dearly all the rest of his life.
In February, just before his eleventh birthday, the
inevitable summons came. A place had been booked
for him on the London coach and he was to return
at once. He felt heartbroken at the news and obeyed
with many tears. Giles gave him as a parting present a
set of *The Bee*, Oliver Goldsmith's magazine, " a mis-

cellany of essays on the most interesting and entertaining subjects." Charles enjoyed every word of it
and used it later as a model of what such a magazine
should be, when he planned *Master Humphrey's Clock*
and *Household Words*.

Dickens wrote his own description of that departure
from Chatham on a dismally wet day, himself the
only inside passenger traveling in the coach, his legs
wrapped with straw to keep them warm. It felt to him
unpleasantly as though he were being forwarded to
his parents, like a parcel postpaid! He munched his
sandwiches miserably. Fond as he was of his family—
and this cannot be doubted—he plainly had no desire
to return to them, and felt nothing but grief and resentment at having to do so. His father met him at the
coach station, and took him home. The house was much
the same size as their last in Chatham, newly built
among the fields and farmlands of Camden Town
across which London was only just beginning to spread.
There were coaches running into town, but most of
the people who lived there were clerks and city workers
(like Bob Cratchit in *The Christmas Carol*) who could
not afford to ride, but walked to their work—as Charles
himself did a few months later.

He found the little place bare and comfortless, and
the nine-year-old orphan was a poor exchange for
capable Mary Weller as maid of all work. Charles was
given an attic, looking over fields. (Its tiny window is
now preserved in Dickens House in Doughty Street,
London.) Water came from a pump in the street, almost opposite their door. There was a night police-
man's box just down the road. A laundress lived next
door, and made candy in her spare time.

The road was muddy, with big puddles spreading

across it in wet weather. It was strewn with household refuse, cabbage stalks, potato peelings, broken crockery and old pots and pans.

Charles was coldly received by his parents. No interest was shown in his progress at school. Nothing at all was said of any further schooling for him though great plans were afoot for Fanny—and she only a girl, for whom education was unusual in those days. She was musical, it seemed and, through a friend of the family who was a piano tuner, had obtained a scholarship at the Academy of Music. Two months after Charles' return, she left home to spend four years there. Charles, meanwhile, was expected to clean his fathers' boots, mind the baby, run errands for his mother and make himself generally useful at home. It says much for his good heart that he was still able to rejoice with Fanny though he wept for himself. Looking back on those days he wrote, "As I thought in the little back garret in Bayham Street of all I had lost in leaving Chatham, what would I have given—if I had had anything to give—to have been sent back to *any* other school, to have been taught *something* anywhere."

Fanny was twelve and a half. She worked hard and with some success, making friends with young musicians, some of whom became famous. She escaped much of the misery Charles now experienced, as when importunate debt collectors shouted at the door and there was no money to pay them. From being the Academy's clever boy with fine prospects, he found himself the household drudge, sharing the life of the little orphan on almost equal terms.

~~~~~~~~~~~~~~~~~~~~~~~~~~~~~~~~~~~~~~

CHAPTER III

A Factory Hand at Twelve

AS THE WEEKS CRAWLED BY AND IT BECAME CLEAR THAT his parents had no idea of sending him back to school, Charles grew sick at heart. He tried to remember what he had learned at Chatham, but he had no text books to remind him and, though he used to say over the Latin verbs and declensions, without teacher or book he was never certain whether he was repeating them correctly.

For consolation he turned to exploring London, eager to find out whether it was anything like what he had imagined from the romantic stories he had read. He particularly longed to see Covent Garden, the big open fruit and vegetable market. So one morning early he crept out and found his way there as the wagons and donkey carts came clattering in over the cobblestones with loads of vegetables and fruit. The reality was much more exciting than he had imagined. He listened to farmers talking, and to the fruit peddlers. He watched the porters swaying by, balancing soaring piles of baskets on their heads. He sniffed at the doors of the eating houses. For Charles Dickens, learning his London was quite as important as anything he might have been taught in a school.

James Lamert was still with the Dickens', idle, for the commission had not yet materialized, and he was glad to play big brother and show Charles some of the sights. He chose some bad parts of the town and made Charles' flesh creep with his tales, warning him what might happen to anyone foolish enough to wander there alone with a clean polite face and decent clothes on his back. They visited the Rookery of St. Giles, a clutter of old houses round the church of St. Giles in the Fields, and stood for a while to watch the pigs and fowls rooting and pecking in the filth of the roadway, and the cages of singing birds which covered the walls of the houses.

In broad daylight the place was quiet but sinister looking. At night the houses would be packed to bursting point with tramps and beggars, filthy, disreputable and abandoned beyond belief. A night's lodging in the Rookery cost anything from a penny to a shilling (twenty-five cents). For the top price, though a bed might be had, it would be filthy and had to be shared with as many more as the proprietor thought fit. On the floor as many men and women as could be squeezed in lay like sardines in a tin, for a penny or so. There might be seventeen people sharing one small, stinking room. When the houses were full, a "crib with straw" could be had in the yards at the back for about three cents a night.

Nurses used to frighten naughty children with tales of kidnapping and baby-snatching, and they did not invent them! Such things happened every day.

Close to the Rookery lay another slum area, Seven Dials—the district in front of the Cambridge Theater —the meeting place of seven streets where a pillar used to stand with a dial pointing down each. It was the home of the printers of the lurid street ballads and broadsides which sold like hot cakes after a murder.

Seven Dials

One of the streets running off it was Monmouth Street, the great haunt of old-clothes men who had only to cast half an eye over a boy to know to the last cent what his clothes were worth.

Charles held on to James very tightly as he stared about him, taking in a great deal more than he then understood though he felt he was looking at such awful wickedness that a deep horror possessed him. Yet the place fascinated him too, and he went back again and again to look at it. Did he see Fagin there and the Artful Dodger and Bill Sikes? He easily may have.

His excursions that summer were not all so terrifying. He had an uncle, Tom Barrow, a brother of his mother's, who was laid up with a broken leg in Gerrard Street, Soho. Uncle Tom was glad of company and Charles dropped in quite often. A bookseller's widow who lived downstairs used to let him in, and loaned him books to read. His uncle had an odd French barber who came in to shave him and talked a great deal about Napoleon and his fatal mistakes, as people today might talk about the way Hitler lost the war in the end. Charles was so fascinated that he tried to write a description of the barber. Thirty years later he described him again in *A Tale of Two Cities*.

One of Charles' godfathers was an oar- and block-maker and rigger for the Navy, with a little shop on the waterfront at Limehouse, near Ropemakers' Fields. It was a long walk to Mr. Huffam's from Camden Town but, as it took him through the City, it never seemed too far for Charles. And so he made his first acquaintance with the little wooden midshipman in Threadneedle Street, which remained such a landmark that when he was famous he still used to stroke its outstretched leg as he went by.

Monmouth Street, haunt of old-clo' men

Wherever he went, Charles gathered fresh, lively impressions of places and people, and of queer happenings and the strangenesses of everyday life.

The old "spasm" still troubled him and he often spent wretched days in bed and worried about what would become of them all. James made him a model theater to while away the time, and they worked on that happily for hours together, making up plays.

It did not take much shrewdness to see that Mr. Dickens' affairs had gone from bad to worse. Debt collectors constantly hung about the house, banging and kicking the front door, shouting up at the windows or through the letterbox, telling him to come down and pay them like an honest man. What Charles felt, he described very clearly in *David Copperfield* when he wrote of the household of the Micawbers and those trips to the pawnbroker's shop. Mrs. Micawber when she declared "If Mr. Micawber's creditors *will not* give him time, they must take the consequences. Blood cannot be obtained from a stone, neither can anything be obtained at present from Mr. Micawber," must have been the genuine echo of his own silly mother.

Naturally, Charles did not understand exactly what it all meant. He thought his father very ill-used, and had no idea how his parents had strained the generosity of their friends to the limit of endurance, never attempting to repay loans, making no personal sacrifice to clear up old debts or to avoid running up new ones. Mr. Dickens was always so sublimely confident that good fortune was just around the corner that it probably seemed to him absurd and undignified to go without the little things he enjoyed, even when he could not pay for them.

At this point, James gave up all thought of the

Army and, instead, went into business with a cousin who had bought a shoe polish factory. He left Bayham Street, and so even that small contribution to the Dickens' budget ceased.

Then Mrs. Dickens thought of mending the family fortunes by opening a school. She expected Mr. Huffam's "maritime" connection to be useful in persuading parents who had to go abroad to leave their children in her charge. She took a large house in Gower Street and moved in immediately with the little furniture which had not yet been pawned or sold. There was so little that most of the rooms had to remain empty. Mr. Dickens drew up the announcement, and his colorful style no doubt made it good reading. When it had been printed, Charles was sent out to slip copies in the letterboxes of all the houses in the neighborhood. He did it after dark, hoping no one would see him, but the prospect gave him hope that at last he would be able to learn something again. A large brass plate inscribed *Mrs. Dickens' Establishment* was ordered and fixed to the front door—but not paid for. No other preparations were made, no classrooms were arranged, no teachers engaged, no courses planned— and no pupils ever came. There was not so much as one inquiry. Very soon the man who had engraved the plate and put it up, came and took it away again.

In this dreary atmosphere Charles' twelfth birthday came round, and James dropped into the cold house to wish him "many happy returns." Seeing how things were, he made what he probably thought the most sensible suggestion in his power. He invited Charles to come and work in his cousin's factory and offered to teach him as much of accounting as he knew himself, though that was not much. He promised

six or seven shillings (about $1.50) a week pay, and
surely that would be better than nothing. Plenty of
boys then went out to work long before twelve, and
fell into worse jobs; but to Charles the proposal seemed
to blot out forever his dream of a future. He would
receive no more education once he became a factory
hand. He watched his mother's beaming face and listened to her rhapsodies with a very sore heart. She
and his father could not have seemed more pleased,
he thought, if he had won a scholarship to a university.

He was to work twelve hours a day, six days a
week, at the blacking factory, as it was called. Charles
described the warehouse where he worked as "a crazy,
tumbledown old house abutting on the river and
literally over-run with rats" with "wainscotted rooms
and rotten floors and staircase," and "the old gray
rats swarming down in the cellars" with "the sound of
their squeaking and scuffling coming up the stairs at
all times." C340281 CO. SCHOOLS

His work was to label little bottles of blacking and
to fit paper tops on them so that they looked as smart
as bottles of medicine from the druggist. At first he had
a table in the office on the first floor under James'
eye, and a boy from the basement brought up his
materials and showed him what to do. Looking at him,
Charles wondered if this was what he also would come
to, so poor, rough and ill-kempt, no different at first
sight from the boys he had watched in Seven Dials.
Having started with such high hopes, it was hard to
have to take instructions now from one he thought
so far beneath him, an illiterate boy in ragged dirty
apron and paper cap. He was more humiliated when
he found that, try as he would, he could not do the
job as well as the others. They worked more quickly

and neatly, gummed their labels on squarely, tied the string tight and trimmed away the paper caps evenly around the bottle's neck.

James, on his high stool behind a glass partition with his ledgers before him, watched Charles fumble with scissors and paper and found him unresponsive. He was only free to teach him during the lunch hour and, as Charles did not seem to be appreciating all that was being done for him, James soon gave up trying. A few mornings later, Charles found his table moved down to the basement where the other boys worked. He might have come off badly there, for his "little gentleman" airs were resented, but Bob Fagin, who had been his instructor, took him under his wing. Bob had a simple admiration for him because he could read and write and always looked so clean and neat. Charles took it all for granted; yet it was from Bob that he first recognized the difference between the roughness of manners which came from hardship and lack of education, and the toughness he so feared in the street boys who had become accustomed, almost from infancy, to a life of crime and violence.

Once, over their work, Charles gave one of his old recitations—gestures, attitudes and all—and was taken aback by their furious resentment. These things made a deep impression on him so that, even after he was married and succeeding as an author, he used to dream of them and wake in a sweat of misery. He never spoke of them to anyone until he began to think of writing *David Copperfield*.

Events at home came swiftly to a head, and about two weeks after Charles had begun work, his father was arrested for a debt of forty pounds ($200). The house was in an uproar. Mrs. Dickens had hysterics, John

Dickens wept and made speeches. Charles was kept
from work to run about with letters begging for loans,
however small. He, poor boy, thought the end of the
world had come when he saw his father taken away,
declaring, as he went, that the sun had set forever
upon his unhappy head. Charles looked anxiously at
the rest of the family. His own small wages would not
go far towards buying food for them, let alone keeping
a roof over their heads—but he need not have distressed
himself. Mr. Dickens soon found it was not such a
calamity after all to be shut away in the Marshalsea
Prison, for no debt collectors could get at him; and it
was quite customary for wives to join their husbands
there. So Mrs. Dickens very quickly arranged to do so,
taking the younger children with her. She rented a
room outside the prison gates for the orphan and
found a place for Charles to live. The queer conditions
in the Marshalsea are described both in *David Copperfield* and *Little Dorrit*.

Charles' new home was in Camden Town, in a sort
of lodging house for children kept by the woman he
later described as Mrs. Pipchin in *Dombey and Son*,
"an ill-favored, ill-conditioned woman" in whom there
was "no milk of human kindness nor gladness" and
who had a face "mottled like bad marble, a beak nose
and a hard gray eye." He shared a room there with
two other boys, but had to buy his own food out of
his wages and look after himself entirely. He thought
no one cared to speak to him—probably it was because
he had to get up earlier than the rest and was too
tired at night for anything but supper and bed.

He bought his food for the day each morning,
milk, bread, cheese, and ate one loaf and a cup
of milk for breakfast, and the same, with a piece of

cheese, for supper. He was always hungry and greatly tempted by the stale pastry at reduced prices which he used to see laid out in Tottenham Court Road as he walked to work. To buy them, however, would mean going hungry later on. He had not money for both. To eke it out, he used to divide his wages into six parts, one for each day of the week, and wrap each separately in paper. For his dinner he generally laid out his few pennies on suet pudding (a steamed pastry made with beef or mutton fat) at one of the cheap eating houses off the Strand. He was allowed half an hour off for tea. If he had no money for food, he took a turn in Covent Garden and stared at the pineapples. If he could afford it, he went to a coffee-shop for coffee and a slice of bread and butter. He recalled, long afterwards, how he used to go to one in St. Martin's Lane, and often sat staring at the glass door which had "Coffee Room" inscribed on it outside in white letters. From his seat, the words became *mooR eeffoC*, which he used to repeat under his breath with dismal satisfaction, "Moor eeffoc, moor eeffoc, moor eeffoc."

CHAPTER IV

At Home in the Marshalsea

EVERY SUNDAY MORNING CHARLES WENT TO FETCH FANNY
and escorted her to Southwark to spend the day with
the family. What they said to one another—Fanny so
well provided for, Charles so hopeless and forlorn—on
those long walks through the City and across the river
has never been told. He probably put a good face on
it. He certainly kept his troubles to himself, and no
hard feelings grew between them for they remained
lifelong friends and allies.

As soon as the warden had let them through the
great gates, Charles forgot everything else in his eagerness to see more of the strange pattern of life within.
Being debtors, not law-breakers, the "Collegians" (as
he called them in *Little Dorrit*) enjoyed a certain
freedom. Quarters of a kind were provided, not cells
and, at a small charge, there was hot water and a
fire to cook by. The degree of comfort depended on
what ready money the prisoners could produce. Mr.
Dickens, with his regular civil service pay, was very
comfortable. He had no rent and was making no effort
to settle any of his debts now that there were no
debt collectors at his heels. Prisoners could not leave
the prison, though wives and families could and did.

Mr. Dickens enjoyed the life and his buoyancy
was refreshing to older inhabitants who lived chiefly

39

Debtors and their friends in the yard at the Marshalsea

on false hopes. They gathered around him admiringly, and his condescension was gracefully done. He was soon the most popular man there, and gave a tone to the place with his little maidservant running in as soon as the gates were opened (and that was at six in the morning) to cook and clean and run errands, and to look after the children.

In *Little Dorrit* the "father of the Marshalsea" was the oldest inhabitant. Mr. Dickens' distinction may have been that he was the richest among them. He always behaved as though he were staying for a time, entirely of his own free will, and as an honored guest, in a pleasant residential club. He greeted his son and daughter benignly on their weekly visits and presented them formally to his fellow "guests." He talked a great deal and with an air of eloquence, allowing a cough to interrupt the flow whenever he lost the thread of his discourse—as that was after every few words, much of it was meaningless. Yet even Charles admired the sound, while the Collegians listened with enthusiasm.

Mrs. Dickens also talked much and to little purpose. But she was an excellent mimic and kept the children in fits of laughter with her imitations of the odd characters about the place.

The birthday of King George IV was celebrated in June and that year Mr. Dickens conceived the great idea of getting up a petition for a grant of money with which to drink His Majesty's health. With his civil service experience he was in his element composing this noble plea, and a day was appointed for the debtors to sign it. The enterprise was spoken of so solemnly that Charles begged permission to be present and received it, provided he could obtain leave of absence from his work. This he did, of course, and on

the great day, was tucked into a corner from which he
could see all that went on without getting in the way.

He watched the scene with the liveliest appreciation. His father, as Chairman of the Debtors' Management Committee, was much in evidence. A long tail
of paper for the signatures was spread out on an
ironing board, which did duty at night as someone's
bed. A Captain Porter stood by, ready and anxious to
read out the high-sounding phrases to anyone who
showed the slightest willingness to listen. Out of his
mouth, the phrases *Your Majesty, Your gracious Majesty, Your Gracious Majesty's unfortunate subjects,*
rolled sonorously to the delight of Mr. Dickens, listening as Charles said "with a little of the author's
vanity." Charles thought often about the scene, and
when he described Mr. Pickwick in the Fleet Prison,
he used it and believed he hardly missed out "half
a dozen men from the Marshalsea crowd."

At first Charles had really thought his father would
die of shame at being in the debtors' prison. He was
glad it was not so, but his relief was cold comfort
as he saw how indifferent in their turn his father and
mother were to his own situation. They seemed not to
regard him as their young son, but as some fortunate
young man, sparing a day out of a free, full life to
visit them. When they said goodbye on Sunday nights,
they expected his pity but had none for him, going
back to loneliness and drudgery. It was all very well
to keep his troubles to himself and to bear them brave-
ly, but this pretense that his life was a bed of roses
wore him down. He was hungry, and nobody cared.
He was often very frightened, and nobody even knew
that there was anything to be frightened of.

During most of the six long working days he felt

terribly alone and abandoned. Then one Sunday when it was time to go, he flung himself on his father's shoulder and wept. Mr. Dickens was taken aback. He was touched and his chest swelled with sentimental pride, but he was too surprised to hide the fact that he had not the slightest clue to what it was all about. Still Charles told him nothing, only cried and said he was lonely and wanted to be with the family—a very right state of mind, no doubt Mr. Dickens felt. With a cough and a few inarticulate words it was conveyed to Charles that something would be done. The orphan had a lodging outside the prison. Mrs. Dickens would find one for her son.

Only a few minutes' walk from the gates was Lant Street, in which a little room was found for him in a clean, pleasant house with pleasant, simple people. A mattress and bedding were sent from the Dickens' own quarters and Charles was installed there within the week. In spite of the picture he drew of that street in *Pickwick Papers* when he lodged Bob Sawyer and the other medical students there, Charles was happy there and remembered the atmosphere when he drew kind Mrs. Garland in the *Old Curiosity Shop*.

It was early summer when Charles moved into his new room. He liked to get up early and run down to the river before the prison gates were open. The orphan often joined him. They lingered by London Bridge, watching the boats and the wharves, and looking downstream to the Tower. Sometimes he invented blood-curdling stories about them for her.

The gates closed each night at ten, but Charles was usually back in his lodging before nine. He thought himself in paradise after the bleakness of Mrs. Roylance's boarding house. Now he took his lunch to work in a red cotton handkerchief and often had a penny or two to spare at the end of the week for presents, a magazine, or a sort of imitation coffee much used then by those who could not afford the genuine article. Occasionally he stopped to look at peepshows and menageries where he saw "the Fat Pig, Wild Indian and the little Lady." He wandered into "little low-browed old shops" looking for treasures. He told in *David Copperfield* how one day he ventured into a public house and ordered himself a glass of beer— "the Genuine Stunning"—*with a good head on it,"* though he was hardly tall enough to see over the counter.

The death of his mother brought John Dickens' days in the Marshalsea to an end. She had left him part of her savings, though only half as much as to his brother William, on account of his numerous loans. William immediately paid into Court the money necessary to secure John's release—for which John was not at all grateful as it meant facing his impatient creditors again.

The cheers at the farewell party from fellow prisoners must have rung hollowly in Mr. Dickens' ear. He and his family passed in triumph through the gates and hurried to Mrs. Roylance's, where they lived until a house could be found. There was a new baby, Augustus, and the little orphan must have had her hands full.

Perhaps the most pressing of Mr. Dickens' problems was to discover how he stood with the Navy Pay Office. He felt hesitant about returning to his desk, though he had carefully sent in a doctor's certificate to gloss over his absence. When he found that it was doubtful whether he would be taken back, in spite of having been paid in full while he was away, he pressed the matter of his "disability" and asked optimistically if he might be allowed to retire—on a pension.

The medical certificate had, in fact, offered no grounds for such a step, and he was instructed to remain away from the Office until the authorities could decide what to do with him. At length, in consideration of twenty years' service and his responsibilities as husband and father of six young children, he was retired with an annual pension of £145 (about $2,175). He was frankly delighted.

His next move was surprising. It appeared that he had picked up a smattering of shorthand while in prison, enough to get casual employment as a stenographer in the Gallery of the House of Commons. Reporters' work in the House did not start until the afternoon, though it often continued into the small hours of the morning, but the life sounded more to his liking than the regular routine of the Civil Service.

John Henry Barrow, another brother of Mrs. Dickens, may have put this idea into his head, for he had started printing a paper, *The Mirror of Parliament,* containing verbatim reports of the debates in the House. Mr. Dickens' shorthand, however, was not nearly good enough for that paper, which was gaining a reputation for reliability.

From the moment he heard of his father's release from the Marshalsea, Charles waited breathlessly for news of his own future—but none came. It evidently never crossed the mind of either parent to take him away from the blacking factory. Mr. Dickens, with his peculiar gift for boasting, was so accustomed to describing his son's humble occupation as the start of a career of boundless promise that he could not bring his mind down to the reality. He shut his eyes to the look on Charles' face, but fate took a hand.

Lamert and his cousin had taken new premises on the north side of the Strand, and had set Charles to work in a window as an advertisement. Charles made no mention of this at home, but it happened that his father came upon him there unawares as he was strolling with a friend from the Navy Pay Office one lunchtime. The other man recognized the boy in the window and stopped to give him half a crown. Mr. Dickens made no comment. He was too outraged. He was wounded in his vanity. By the time Charles came home his father had worked himself into a fury of indignation. He wrote a stiff letter to be taken to James Lamert next day. Lamert, quite as angry as Mr. Dickens, told Charles that it was impossible to keep him after what had been said. He sent Charles home and, anxious as he was to get away from the detested place, Charles could hardly bear to do so in such circumstances. He wept and then, "with a relief so strange that it was like oppression," left the blacking factory forever.

Mrs. Dickens was not at all pleased at the turn events had taken. She scolded Charles and railed at her husband, then went down to Chandos Street to put matters right herself. She succeeded and returned triumphantly with the news that James would take Charles back as though nothing had occurred.

She had mistaken her husband's feelings, however. Mr. Dickens had been humiliated, grossly humiliated, and before a friend. He was not to be moved. He told her he wished to hear no more of the matter. Charles was *not going back*.

~~~~~~

CHAPTER V

On the Way Up

To make up a little Mr. Dickens now proposed in his most genial fashion that, after an absence of nearly eighteen months, Charles should go back to school. He chose Wellington House Academy in Hampstead Road. It was not a good school and Charles did not shine there. "It was remarkable for white mice," he recalled in a note about that part of his life, "and birds—redpolls, linnets and even canaries were kept in desks, drawers, hat-boxes and other strange refuges for birds. But white mice were the favorite stock. The boys trained the mice much better than the masters trained the boys. One lived in the cover of a Latin dictionary. It ran up ladders, drew Roman chariots, shouldered a musket, turned wheels, and even made a very creditable appearance on the stage as the *Dog of Montargis.*" He described this school as Salem House in *David Copperfield.*

Even if the school had been better Charles might not have profited much by it. It was not easy to go back to lessons after such a break as his, spent in such work and company. He found it hard to concentrate, had forgotten most of what he had learned in Latin and mathematics and could not get to grips with them again. He had been William Giles' bright boy. Now he

48 THE STORY OF CHARLES DICKENS

was nobody, just one of the herd, not dull but backward. If he was disappointed, he hardly showed it
and the time at Wellington House served some purpose in giving him a chance to recover his balance a
little and to look ahead.

He may have appeared little different from the
other boys in his pepper-and-salt suit, with its short
jacket and turn-over collar, but he was very much
aware of experiences which properly brought up
schoolboys do not have. The thought, *"What would
they think if they knew?"* often ran through his mind,
and kept him glancing sideways at himself and them.
He tried to behave as they did but he no longer
thought like that, or accepted life on their level. He
felt now that to be whipped would be an unendurable
humiliation, and took care to avoid it. Yet it was hard
to submit himself to school discipline.

He had been a worker, independent in his poor
way, having to plan his own daily life and manage
his money. This curious contrast of which he was so
much aware focused too much of his attention on the
impressions he was making. He wanted badly to shine.
As he could not do so in lessons he thought up a
dozen little tricks to excite the boys' admiration. He
invented a lingo which he made his friends learn.
They used to talk it very fast in the street in the hope
that people would think them foreigners. He found
them a good audience for his stories. They produced
a toy theater and he brought out some of the plays
he and James had made for theirs. He led them into
silly pranks like hanging about Euston Road and
begging from old ladies for the sheer fun of it, coaching them in what to say and how to say it.

He stayed at the school a little more than two years

and learned a poor smattering of Latin, history, mathematics—and the hornpipe. At the end of that time his Uncle William died and left his share of his mother's money to his nephews and nieces, to be divided among them after his wife's death, the amount being about thirteen hundred pounds ($6,500). John Dickens cannot have been pleased. He was always in need of money and just at this time he was being evicted for not paying rent. It was not surprising that Charles left school hurriedly and began to look for a job.

This time he did not mind. Those two years had given him a breathing space in which to think about his future. The old dream of going to a university was dead, of course, but there were other roads to the same goal. He was fifteen and had to start from the bottom, but that did not dismay him. He listened to a good deal of advice on how to begin. He knew enough of a clerk's life in the Civil Service to refuse that. He knew, also, a little about reporting in the House of Commons, and he thought that sounded very good indeed, but he would have to wait for it until he was twenty and make himself an expert at shorthand. His uncle, if not his father's colleagues, must have warned him of that.

His first job came eventually through a connection of his mother's and he became most junior clerk, office boy in fact, to a lawyer of Symonds Inn called Charles Malloy.

This was the beginning of his intimate knowledge of lawyers' offices which inspired the famous scenes in *Pickwick, Bleak House,* etc. He parodied the lawyer's clerks amusingly in *Pickwick Papers,* describing his own position at Symonds Inn as that of one of "the

Clerks on their high stools in a lawyer's office

office lads in their first surtouts," blithely scorning
boys still at school and clubbing together on their way
home to buy sausages and porter, cheerfully certain
that "there's nothing like life."

Charles had little enough to do there, but he was
already watching the types which frequented the office. He learned their histories, and stored up all he
saw for that future which was so much nearer than
anyone could have guessed, seeing him on his high
stool, not trusted with any work which might have
required the slightest output of intelligence or initia-
tive.

He stayed at Mr. Malloy's a bare six weeks, and
then moved on to another lawyer's office, to Ellis and
Blackmore's of Gray's Inn, leaving a lifelong friend
in the first, a fellow clerk called Tom Mitton. The new
post was not much better, but started with thirteen
shillings a week which was increased after a month's
trial to fifteen. The notebook in which he entered his
accounts in that office still exists. When Charles had
become famous, Mr. Blackmore fancied he recognized
incidents and characters in *Pickwick* and *Nickleby*
which had grown out of happenings in his office.

The work there made so little demand on him
that Charles started to study shorthand. He spent
ten shillings ($2.50) on Gurney's *Brachygraphy,* as it
was then called. He started cheerfully enough, but was
soon in despair, then in turns dogged, defiant, determined. He wrote in *David Copperfield* of the nightmare of dots, circles and "marks like flies' legs" which
he suffered in mastering the alphabet of shorthand,
and of the "horrors called *arbitrary characters.*" He
stuck at it, however, until he had made himself master

of the art. In eighteen months he reached a speed and proficiency rarely achieved in those days, yet he still found time to go about with other boys. They went to the theater, and Charles' early interest flared up into something more so that he chose the plays with care, picking out actors and following their careers from play to play. He tried to be critical, weighing interpretation against what he felt to be the author's intention. He revelled in argument with his friends after the play was over.

In those days extras for crowd scenes were often engaged for the night at the stage door, and Charles took the opportunity to learn what it felt like to be out on a stage. He found it exciting and, however tawdry the atmosphere, the feeling of romance remained with him. Once he was given a line to speak. He found to his great chagrin that he could hardly get the words out, but he began to see himself as an actor.

All this time his family was still living in furnished rooms, which they changed every few months. In spite of perpetual difficulties over money they seem to have kept a pleasant atmosphere in the home. Fanny was back with them, and beginning to earn a living with her music. Charles contributed a shilling or two when he managed to keep them from his father. On Saturday evenings they were sociable, and entertained their friends. Fuel and wine were cheap, and there would always be a roaring fire for the young folk to gather round, home-brewed punch with pies and cooked meats from the pastrycooks, and perhaps a bunch of cheap cigars or cheroots for the men. Fanny's friends provided music and there was much lively talk. Sometimes they danced or acted charades. Mr. and Mrs.

Dickens were at their best on these occasions: he, magnificently urbane, she, the mistress of all genteel airs and graces.

The disadvantage of Mr. Dickens' employment as a political reporter was that his engagements were intermittent, for both the work and pay of stenographers ceased while Parliament was in recess. The longest vacation was in the summer with a good three months to be tided over. John Dickens did not worry much about that. It offered a plausible excuse for his incessant borrowings, and he liked the irregular life. But, of course, his load of debt grew, and evading his creditors became quite an occupation in itself.

Fanny's and Charles' earnings were still small, and Charles often felt uneasy as he looked from the "prodigal parent" to the younger children still dependent on him. He gave them all the money he could spare and took his share of responsibility in all their troubles. Incidentally, he took to heart the object lesson, and was convinced that only misery came of failing, as Mr. Micawber was to say, to match income to expenditure.

He stayed with Ellis and Blackmore for the eighteen months it took him to master shorthand; then gave notice. The normal rate of promotion of clerks in lawyers' offices was too slow for him, and he had now qualified himself for something better. A cousin put the idea into his head of trying his luck as a stenographer at Doctors' Commons. That meant renting a "box" there where he put up his card and waited for work. Neither the Court nor the building still exists. It was near St. Paul's Churchyard where the Doctors of Civil Law "commoned" together and

administered ecclesiastical law, probate, marriages and
divorces, and disputes connected with ships and boats.
Stenographers were needed to take down verbatim
the evidence of witnesses. Charles proved quick and
reliable, and soon had as much work as he could do.
Thus, at sixteen, he successfully made his first bid for
independence and added greatly to the experience
which went to make him so great a writer.

In Doctors' Commons he saw another side of the
law. He met in real life some of the tyrannical, crafty
old lawyers he put into his books, and learned to
hate and distrust them. He watched the helplessness
of simple, honest men at the mercy of these professional tricksters with their desk thumping and vio-
lent hectoring voices, and realized the corruption that
passed for justice and the law. The most desirable
sort of business there, he said in *David Copperfield,*
was "a good case of a disputed will . . . some neat little
estate of thirty or forty thousand pounds" . . . good
for "pickings" at every stage of the proceedings until
nothing was left for the heirs. Another sidelight on
the activities of the Courts was put into Sam Weller's
lips, in *Pickwick,* in connection with Tony Weller's
second marriage and the license peddlers.

~~~~~~~~~~~~~~~~~~~~~~~~~~~~~~~~

CHAPTER VI

First Love and New Ambitions

LITTLE DID THE LAWYERS WHO EMPLOYED CHARLES AS stenographer realize what weapons they were putting into his hands. They set him to take down, word for word, the evidence of their witnesses, and displayed before him the tricks and dodges by which they deceived and defrauded their clients. What did not go into the written record was kept just as safely in that reliable memory of his. He must often have cast his mind back to these scenes when he was looking for the right note and authentic words to use in one of his stories.

What he saw there put him for life on the side of the simple man, usually so ignorant of the law and so little protected by it in those days. He felt angrily that "the Law put all honest men under the diabolical hoofs of all the scoundrels."

Within the next fifty years, the legal profession brought about their own reforms from within, and some credit for it must be given to Charles for putting ordinary people on their guard, and showing them how necessary and overdue an overhaul was.

He was growing up and thinking seriously now about Life, trying to make up his mind what mattered, what he believed in, examining everyday principles and standards of behavior, and trying to decide what he was prepared to stand by. He hammered it out in fierce arguments with his friends, shouting a good deal because of the strength of his feelings and because their hesitancy or indifference made him impatient. With a fundamental honesty and feeling for truth he challenged all insincerity and humbug, often with unnecessary violence.

A new belief in himself was growing, and new hopes of the future. He could not help knowing that the concentration which he had put into learning shorthand was rare among the young men he knew, and was admired. He realized that he had brains, but he still wondered anxiously whether lack of education would keep him down, though he had no longer the old feeling of resentment because school had been denied him when he wanted it so passionately. Now he set out to see what he could do for himself. First he must learn some history and much more of the literature of his own and possibly other countries, but he had no money to buy books, and the kind of library he needed was not open to him. Then he discovered that as soon as he was eighteen he would be able to use the Reading Room at the British Museum. That settled his main difficulty. He applied for a ticket early, so that it was in his hands on the morning of his eighteenth birthday. He drew up schemes of study and, though they were ambitious, he stuck to them. He tackled this reading in his usual headlong fashion, tearing the heart out of one book after another, making rapid notes as he read, yet digesting a good deal.

He did not hope to make up in this way for all a university would have done for him. He was a realist, taking life as it came and making the best of it. John

Forster, a lawyer and literary critic who became his most important friend and wrote the life of him to which all other biographers have to turn for much of their material, said that no one who knew him in his later life and discussed books and ideas with him would ever have suspected that his schooldays had been "so scrambling and haphazard."

Forster thought that what contributed most to Dickens' success was perhaps the attitude to life which came from the mouth of David Copperfield when he said, "What I have tried to do in life, I have tried with all my heart to do well. What I have devoted myself to, I have devoted myself to completely. Never to put one hand to anything on which I could throw my whole self, and never to affect depreciation of my work whatever it was."

It was in this frame of mind that he presently considered going on the stage. He had discovered that he had quite a special gift for slipping into the skin of another person—a trick helped by his vivid memory and by his intense interest in other people and used already in his clever way of telling a story. Looking into himself, he believed that he had in him the makings of an actor, and the thought excited him. He began to study acting parts, though without abandoning his reading plans, and he learned many by heart. He found an actor to give him lessons in the art of deportment and learned how to enter and leave a room gracefully, how to sit down and get up, to bow gracefully, practicing each lesson diligently before a mirror.

He was not mistaken about having a talent for acting. His later life proved it, but at the time he could not trust it. Perhaps he could not see how to live until the time when his talent might be recognized. If he threw away what he had built up with his one sure qualification—shorthand—what would he have to fall back on in bad times? He hesitated, and let the idea drop. The lessons in deportment were not wasted. They stood him in good stead a few years later, when the houses of the great were opened to welcome him as a lion of the literary world.

Among those who gathered at the Dickens' on Saturday nights were some who were to make names for themselves as composers and singers. Led by Charles, with his interest in the stage, his high spirits and enthusiasm, they wrote operettas, plays and charades which they produced very seriously, hiring costumes and rehearsing as earnestly as though they were preparing to perform at Covent Garden Theater. Even Mr. and Mrs. Dickens and young Augustus were pressed into service and took small parts. Hardly anyone was left over to be the audience. John Hullah was their best composer, and among the performers was a young architect, Henry Austin, who in time married Letitia Dickens, and Henry Kolle, a great friend of Charles, who was a calico printer in the City.

Kolle admired Charles very much. He was in love with a girl and became engaged to her about that time. He could not rest until he had brought Charles to see her. Her name was Anne Beadnell. She had two sisters: the older one, Margaret, already engaged to a tea merchant; the younger, Maria. Her father was manager of a bank. They were a fairly typical middle-class family of the period, snobbish, rather stupid and very materialistic. The daughters were always strictly chaperoned and any young man who came to the house had to face a searching examination as to

his family and prospects. When Charles was introduced by Kolle, he had to parry the questions he
could not answer candidly—and there was a good deal
he did not wish to admit at first meeting—his father's
financial condition, for instance.

Slim, nervous, vivacious, he did not make a good
impression on Mrs. Beadnell. As soon as the first restraint wore off he became much too talkative, told
too many jokes and stories of the Courts, and told
them too theatrically, mimicking the voices of the
various parties altogether too cleverly. He set the girls
tittering and giggling. Mrs. Beadnell thought him loud
and altogether too odd a personality for her daughters. She snubbed him heavily and disparaged his
family—but the damage had been done. Charles had
given one look at Maria, and fallen headlong in love
with her.

She was about twelve months older than Charles,
a silly, arch little creature who loved nothing so much
as playing off one admirer against another while she
sat back genteelly enjoying their discomfiture, and
working up romantic little tales to amuse her girl
friends. She seems to have had no heart to speak of,
none for Charles certainly, and showed a mean, ill-
natured disposition. She was immensely tickled by his
extravagant conversation, and the desperate passion
which he soon showed all too clearly made her scream
with laughter. She made a fool of him and enjoyed
doing it—but still he loved her with all his boyish
ardor. He thought of her day and night. He took to
haunting the neighborhood on the mere chance of
catching a glimpse of her. He even loitered beneath
her windows at night, staring up at them and dream-

ing goodness knows what foolishness, and that only made her laugh the more.

His first love jerked him out of the last phases of boyhood, and he grimly faced the mockery and her parents' disparagement alike. He determined to make himself quickly a position that would make them respect and welcome him. He did not dream of the heights of fame to which he actually came, but he saw no reason why he should not do as well at least as Kolle or Margaret's fiancé. He thought he had done pretty well already in getting away from the clerks' rut and in making a place for himself in Doctors' Commons. But his ambition did not stop at being a successful stenographer and, if that was not good enough for the Beadnells, he was prepared to produce something more dramatic. It was never Charles' way to wait for things to turn up. He had seen too much of that in his father's life. He made them happen, and now his ambition leaped ahead, feeling the spur.

He had had little experience of safe, respectable home life where debts and debt collectors had not to be considered. The solid comfort which he saw at the Beadnells must have seemed very attractive to him. It was a safe setting for Maria! Probably he never saw her as she really was. He watched the sisters making music, Maria playing the harp with little airs and graces which seemed to him entrancing. She knew every trick of coquetry. She had a little dog—the very one Charles described as Dora's in *David Copperfield*. She used it much as Dora did, as a fence between them.

The conventions demanded that the Beadnell and the Dickens parents should exchange visits. It is hardly to be expected that the City folk would not sum up

John Dickens pretty shrewdly—and Mrs. Dickens' housekeeping, too. That would fill in for Mrs. Beadnell all she wanted to know of the family's background. She must have felt sure she was right in her determination to let nothing develop between their son and her daughter. She let Charles come to the house, but made it intolerably clear that he could never be considered eligible for the hand of a Beadnell daughter. He probably would not have been welcome there at all, but for his knack of making a party go. He described one of these Beadnell entertainments in a long rhyme which he called *The Bill of Fare*. It described those present in terms of some dish and ended with epitaphs on them. Mr. Beadnell was "a good fine sirloin of beef"; his wife, "an excellent rib of the same"; while Anne and Maria were "two nice little ducks and very well dressed." As for himself, he was "a young summer cabbage without any heart"—having lost his "a twelve month ago from last May." This went down very well with the girls, whatever their parents thought about it!

Now, in his desire to prove himself, Charles gave earnest thought to his career. He was nineteen, and would be eligible for work as a reporter in the House of Commons on his next birthday. This had seemed to him a notable landmark on the road to success, but would even that be enough for the Beadnells? He was terribly afraid of losing Maria altogether, and longed to pull off something really spectacular! Names could be made overnight in the theater. Could even Mrs. Beadnell hold out against him if he had fame, position and money to show?

Thinking thus, he took his courage in both hands and composed a letter to the stage manager of the

Covent Garden Theater, a Mr. Bartley, asking for an appointment. He described the circumstances later (to Forster) in a letter which said:

"I wrote to Bartley and told him how young I was, and exactly what I thought I could do, and that I believed I had a strong perception of character and oddity, and a natural power of reproducing in my own person what I observed in others. I recollect that I wrote the letter from a little office I had at Doctors' Commons, where the answer came also.

"There must have been something in my letter that struck the authorities, for Bartley wrote to me almost immediately to say that they were busy getting up *The Hunchback*, but that they would communicate again with me in a fortnight.

"Punctual to the time, another letter came with an appointment to do anything of Mather's I pleased before him and Charles Kemble, on a certain day in the theater. My sister Fanny was in the secret, and was to go with me to play the songs.

"I was laid up when the day came with a terrible bad cold and inflammation of the face. See how near I may have been to another sort of life!"

It was a bold step and his mind must have been in a turmoil as he waited for the day to come. Was he wise to throw away all he had put into his present job, to start afresh with nothing in his pocket, no one behind him, only ambition and his own blind belief in himself to support him? It is understandable that when the fatal day came he was unwell and unable to keep the appointment. He was given the chance of another appointment, but he never took it up.

Before he had made up his mind, however, another · door opened and he had the opportunity he wanted, of

going into the Gallery of the House of Commons*
as official political reporter to a newspaper called *The
True Sun*. He took the chance, and bent all his mind
on succeeding in the new work. It started in March
with the Easter recess ahead and consequently the
prospect of four or five weeks without pay while Parliament was on vacation. He was prepared for it, however, and kept on his box at Doctors' Commons, working there in the mornings as his Parliamentary work
did not begin until afternoon.

* Similar to our House of Representatives

~~~~~~~~~~

CHAPTER VII

Reporting in the House of Commons

CHARLES KNEW WHEN HE PLANNED THIS HEAVY TIME-
table of work that it would prevent him from seeing
Maria except at weekends. He was prepared to put up
with that in the hope of being allowed to marry her
in the end. Her mother chose this moment, however,
to pack her off to Paris out of his way. Maria was
delighted and thought it a good joke to go without
telling him. Charles could hardly believe it of her and
went round to Kolle's rooms to pour his heart out and
find what comfort he could. Because of his engagement to Anne, Kolle knew most of what went on at
the Beadnell's, but was probably sworn to silence in
this affair; also he would not have wanted to wound
his friend's feelings by telling him what was the
plain, painful fact.

Charles refused to give up; he simply flung himself
into his work more furiously than ever, determined
to show the Beadnells what he was made of. He drove
himself unsparingly, and snatched at every opportunity that offered. The physical strain was great, but his
feet were safely on the road to success.

He still had no thought of becoming a writer but,
if he had deliberately sought experiences which would
help him in such a career, he could hardly have chosen
anything more fruitful than the Courts of Doctors'

Commons and the House of Commons. The Debates in Parliament gave him a remarkable insight into the conditions in which the poor lived, for it was a time when revolutionary ideas were bursting out on every hand, and the spirit of social as well as political reform was at its liveliest.

He entered the Gallery of the House as a reporter in time to hear one of the biggest programs of reform ever accomplished by any party in Britain in so short a time. The party in power were the Whigs under Lord Grey, and the Reform Bill of 1832 was going through its last stages. Two years later, when Lord Grey resigned, the old Poor Law system had been revised, slavery had been abolished in the British Dominions, and the first really effective factory laws had been made. These included the children's charter. Children under nine were no longer allowed to work in mines or factories, and those between nine and thirteen who were so employed had to attend lessons for at least two hours a day. Also, for the first time, the State was providing funds for education.

The True Sun was a Radical paper. It cost sevenpence (of which fivepence was tax), and any enterprising carrier who rushed copies out to the country could be certain of selling them there for double the London price. The thirst for news was intense, and "news" then meant mainly political news, not sport or crime or gossip. There was not much money to be made out of a newspaper and the owners ran them in the hope of wielding political influence. The greater part of the population was illiterate, but the news was read aloud in inns and taverns and elsewhere to eager gatherings of men. One copy thus served a wide public.

Men were beginning to be aware that it was a handicap not to be able to read. In the North, mechanics' institutes were being opened to provide evening classes to which industrial workers were flocking eagerly. Popular education had begun, and there were 12,000 free public schools already open.

Charles wanted to be a political reporter in the House of Commons partly because that was one of the important new ideas of the age. Publication of accounts of what went on in the House had been permitted by law since 1770 but both Whig and Tory statesmen still resented having the public know what they had said. There was an element, therefore, of excitement in being one of the responsible few admitted to the House for that purpose. With so much opposition in high quarters, such papers as his Uncle's *Mirror of Parliament* called for the best reporters obtainable. [Such reporters today have to have a shorthand speed of 200 words a minute, perfect hearing and a working knowledge of parliamentary procedure and public affairs.]

The vital importance of reliability was shown in the case of Daniel O'Connor, the "liberator of Ireland" who, about this time, had been keeping up a steady complaint of misrepresentation in the press. The reporters for *The Times* at length took the matter up, and sent their editor a round robin declaring that they would not report any more of O'Connell's speeches until he withdrew his accusation. They were supported by all their colleagues in the Gallery and the boycott was so inconvenient that the Irishman had to climb down and admit he was wrong.

Another case occurred later when Charles had obtained a post on his Uncle's paper. Feeling was then running high on questions of rent and taxes in Ireland. Lord Stanley—who was in charge of Irish affairs—made a long and extremely important speech in the House on the Government's policy. On such occasions, when speeches were expected to go on for several hours, the reporters arranged to work in shifts of three-quarters of an hour each. Charles was on for the first and, as it happened, the last shift.

Early next morning, Mr. Barrow was horrified to receive a complaint from Lord Stanley that *The Mirror's* account was grossly inaccurate—except for the beginning and the end. He requested the editor to send round to his house immediately the man responsible for the correct reporting, to take down the whole speech from Lord Stanley's own mouth. If misleading statements reached Ireland, incalculable harm might have been done.

Charles went to Carlton House Terrace feeling gratified, if rather nervous. He was shown into a room in which the morning's papers were scattered everywhere. While he waited, he stood by a table turning some of them over, and reading what other reporters had written of the speech. Presently Lord Stanley put his head round the door and coughed, remarking that he had expected to find the gentleman who had reported part of his speech. He evidently thought Charles looked too young for the part but, being assured that he was the man, began immediately to dictate, walking up and down, declaiming as though he were addressing the House. Sir James Graham, who was working with Lord Stanley at the time, joined them and followed the speech carefully from papers he had in his hand, occasionally correcting a word. Charles' pencil flew. When the new report was sent round for approval, Stanley wrote a warm note of thanks and even Mr. Barrow expressed his appreciation.

The incident left a pleasant taste in Charles' mouth. He wondered whether he might not turn it to good account before his name was once more forgotten, so he wrote to Lord Stanley's private secretary asking if he could help him to get any extra reporting work during Parliamentary vacations. The letter still exists with the notes for reply pencilled across the top. They read, "Not likely have opportunity—should one occur should not hesitate recommend."

John Dickens found life in the Gallery pleasant, and Charles, too, enjoyed the company of his fellow workers. He was well liked for he was modest and rather quiet, conscientious, and always there when he was wanted. Soon they called him affectionately, "the faithful stenographer." He found that, as in Doctors' Commons, he was still able to listen critically without endangering the accuracy of his shorthand. In Parliament he felt as angry and indignant as he had when listening to cases in the Courts. He hated the lack of feeling, the downright dishonesty, indeed, of even some famous speakers.

In the Gallery he heard the whole of the evidence given by the Royal Commission which had been inquiring into the working of the old Poor Law. He felt that their dry accounts gave little impression of the suffering actually inflicted, or of the injury to the pride and dignity of the poor. His sympathy for the simple man had been kindled in the Courts; now he became as strongly the champion of the poor from what he heard in Parliament. O'Connell also touched him deeply with his descriptions of the conditions behind the anti-tax riots in Ireland. Charles was almost blinded by tears as he listened and recorded the speeches. He could not help entering into the human reality of all he heard. He felt other people's suffering almost as though it were his own. All his life he had the feeling, as he looked at poverty and degradation—"There, but for the grace of God, go I."

He heard all types of eloquence in the House, Lord Wellington's, Gladstone's, Macaulay's, Lord John Russell's and Cobbett's. Of them all, it was Lord John Russell whom he most admired and felt to be worth following and, as will be seen later, he was to have that good fortune.

Since reporters were only grudgingly admitted to the House, no arrangements were made for their comfort. There was no Press Gallery as now. The men had simply to make the best of bare permission to occupy the back row of the Strangers' Gallery. They had no desks to write at and a very poor light. Often they could not even hear what was going on on the floor of the Chamber.

Charles gave an account of these conditions in a speech he made at a Press Fund Dinner long after he had become famous. "I have worn out my knees," he told the audience, "by writing on them in the old back row of the old Gallery of the old House of Commons; and I have worn out my feet standing to write in a preposterous pen in the old House of Lords, where we used to be huddled together like so many sheep."

His work with *The True Sun* began in March, 1832. At the end of the summer session of that year, with the prospect before him of neither work nor pay for three long months, he went to his uncle to see if he could do anything for him. Charles knew that *The Mirror of Parliament,* since it only reported the Debates, lapsed during the vacations, but he got a post on it all the same. As one of "Mr. Barrow's men," he could count on being asked to report speeches by Members in the country during vacation, in their constituencies and elsewhere. Money was still tight and uncertain, but it was obvious that he was making good—even his uncle recognized that.

Mr. Barrow was not an attractive or a genial man, but small, dry and pompous, the original of Mr. Spenlowe in *David Copperfield*, and much like him. Charles had no great regard for him, and Mr. Barrow was cautious with his nephew, fearing to lay himself open to renewed attempts at borrowing by his sister and brother-in-law. Charles' parents had no doubt been more of an embarrassment to him so far than a credit, with their everlasting debts and requests for loans which had never been repaid.

In June, Maria Beadnell returned from France and began a secret correspondence with Charles through Kolle's good services. They addressed each other in the high-faluting terms of a cheap novel. Even Charles' covering letters to Kolle were absurdly stiff. "I would really feel some delicacy in asking you again to deliver the enclosed as addressed were it not for two reasons," one ran. "In the first place, you know so well my existing situation that you must be perfectly aware of the general nature of the note, and in the second, I should not have written it (for I should have communicated its contents verbally) were it not that I lost the opportunity of keeping the old gentleman out of the way as long as possible last night. Perhaps you will accompany the delivery by asking Miss Beadnell only to read it when quite alone."

Maria was as heartless, he as lovelorn, as ever. At

night, after the House had adjourned, and he had
transcribed his reports into longhand for the printer
and delivered them to the office of his paper, he often
wandered on towards Lombard Street. There, in the
early hours of those summer mornings, he gazed up
at the windows of the room where she slept, and
sighed despairingly. After breakfast he haunted the
locality, hoping to catch even a glimpse of her. Once
he was fortunate, and ran into her with Anne and
their mother, all dressed in full round cloaks of green
merino, sailing down Cornhill. He accosted them with
one of his best bows, and offered them his escort,
which was most unwillingly accepted. They were on
their way to a dressmaker's in St. Mary Axe and the
girls chattered across their mother's forbidding countenance archly and mysteriously about wedding garments. At the door of the establishment Charles was
sent about his business by Mrs. Beadnell's remarking
with extreme coolness, "*And now,* Mr. Dickin, we will
wish *you,* good morning." She deliberately refused to
learn his name correctly as part of her technique of
discouragement. The shop door opened and he was
left to stare at three squarely turned backs.

Yet—"I hardly ever go into the City," he wrote long
afterwards, "but I walk up an old court at the back of
the Mansion House and come out by the corner of
Lombard Street!"

That autumn, *The True Sun* was doing badly and
he resigned and worked only for his uncle. He felt
confident that he was gaining ground, and he now
took a step which he may have felt as a move towards
matrimony. He took rooms in Cecil Street, Strand
(where David Copperfield experimented with bache-

lor existence), but Charles never enjoyed the ease
and independence he was to bestow on David.

Life there was pleasant while it lasted. He took
to going into the fresh air on Sundays and sometimes
invited Kolle to go with him, perhaps to Hampstead
"to throw a leg over an 'oss." Saturday evenings generally found him at home with his family, and at the
end of the year he went back to live with them.
They were making another move, this time to an apartment over an upholsterer's shop at 18 Bentinck Street.
Letters from Charles show him engaged in seeing that
everything was made ready for their arrival, the chimneys swept, windows cleaned and coal in the cellar.
It must have been a comfortable place for many parties
were held there and at least one performance of amateur theatricals done on a grand scale. Charles was,
as ever, the mainspring, arranging scenes and costumes, coaching actors and taking a leading part himself. Kolle also had a part but, in the last stages of
his engagement to Anne, could think of nothing but
his approaching nuptials and was never there when
wanted for rehearsals.

"The family are busy," Charles scribbled to him,
"the corps dramatic are all anxiety. The scenery is all
completing rapidly, the machinery is finished, the curtain hemmed, the orchestra complete—and the manager grimy!"

It was by a little mischief-making at this performance that the final separation between Charles and
Maria came about. They had met once or twice in
the previous weeks—perhaps by accident, possibly by
design, but certainly without Mrs. Beadnell's knowledge. And, of course, it had been out of the question
for Maria to take part in the play, or even to be

present. She probably made the most to Charles of not being her own mistress in the matter, yet felt some pangs of envy at being outside all the fun. A friend of hers who had been casting an eye on Charles (quite vainly) during rehearsals brought Maria a mischievous story of Charles' "attentions" to her. Maria went off like a rocket and wrote Charles a ridiculous letter accusing him of playing fast and loose with her. She wanted scenes and she had them. Determined to believe the worst, she stormed and raved and would not listen to anything he said, thoroughly enjoying her grievance.

Her sister's wedding to Kolle took place a few days later with Charles as best man. Maria took care not to speak to him and was sent off to Paris again immediately afterwards by her parents. As before, she told Charles nothing of their decision.

This time it was the end for him. He had done everything he could think of to make her listen to reason, and he had nothing on his conscience. He had suffered exaggeratedly throughout the whole affair. He bitterly blamed Maria's friend for malicious gossip. He reproached Fanny for careless words. Now he thrust it all behind him, not merely as experience bought and profited from, but as most bitter suffering to be buried deep, along with his memories of the blacking factory, where no one could ever reach them. They were not to be spoken of by himself or anyone else. Yet he was not daunted by the blow. He did not mean to give in, and his pride and ambition were only strengthened by what had happened. He was blindly determined, as he said, "to ride on—roughshod if need be, smoothshod if that will do—*but to ride on.*"

~~~~~~

CHAPTER VIII

A Story Published

CHARLES CERTAINLY RODE ON, AND ROUGHSHOD OVER HIS troubles; but for his own peace of mind he had to find something to fill the emptiness Maria's final going left in his life. He had dreamed of her, planned for her so exclusively that it was not easy to change the focus of all his thoughts. He was sure he could never forget her. He would have been hurt and indignant if anyone had told him that he would come to despise her, but the immediate necessity was to get her out of his system. He found hard work the best way to do it.

Looking sharply about him, he heard a new venture which attracted him. It was *The Morning Chronicle,* which was being re-launched by a group of Whig City men in opposition to *The Times.* The story behind the move had stirred the newspaper world, and Charles understood that only men with the highest qualifications would be wanted on it.

Until a few years previously *The Morning Chronicle* had in fact been *The Times'* only rival. It still had a considerable reputation though it had lost ground. Now it was to be revived and used as a weapon in the game of party politics.

The story was that the Government had been seriously inconvenienced by attacks in *The Times* against

the provisions of the Poor Law Amendment Bill, then
before the House. The editor of *The Times* was the
famous Thomas Barnes and he was vigorously attack-
ing the Bill's inhuman attitude not only to paupers,
but also to women and children. He considered it
could only "sow seeds of perpetual enmity between
the poor and the rich."

Lord Althorp, for the Government, was so hard
pressed that he came to wonder how the critical voice
could be silenced. He asked the Lord Chancellor in
a note whether they "should declare open war on *The
Times* or attempt peace?"

That note, purloined from the wastepaper basket
of the House of Lords, came anonymously into Barnes'
hands, and he sent a copy of it to the Chancellor,
adding the words: "To make open war, or attempt
peace? What does the gaby [fool] mean?"

After that, it had to be war, and *The Morning
Chronicle* was the Government's chosen weapon. A
thoroughly tough stockbroker was put in as manager.
John Easthope was his name, but he came to be known
to newspaper men as Blasthope! He needed the best
men money could hire, and was ready to pay well.

Charles would have preferred to apply direct to
Easthope, relying on his wits and his reputation for
good work in the Gallery, and asked his uncle for an
introduction. But Mr. Barrow did not quite like to do
that. Instead he sent a note to the man who had been
put in charge of staff appointments (a Mr. Payne
Collier), mildly recommending his nephew, as an "extremely clever youth." That was not poor praise under
the circumstances and Collier inquired about Charles'
background and education—the very thing Charles
wanted to avoid. He knew that, on paper, he had

nothing much to offer. On second thought Mr. Barrow agreed to invite Collier to dinner to meet his nephew and judge for himself.

It proved a most successful evening. Charles was in excellent form, gay, amusing, talkative. He was persuaded to sing some comic songs which went down very well. Collier went back to town satisfied that he could back young Dickens' application without fear of running foul of Easthope. So Charles got the new post at a salary of five guineas a week (equivalent to about $75 now). It was to be paid *all the year round,* but he was not to take it up until the summer of 1834.

(By the way, a sub-editorship on the paper was applied for by a young man whose education and background were entirely beyond suspicion—William Makepeace Thackeray—but he was not successful, and shortly afterwards joined the staff of *The Times.*)

Charles must have considered that he was now well on the way to the top of his little world. He began to wonder whether he could make any extra money by writing. He knew he could tell a story well by word of mouth to the delight of his hearers—but could he get the same liveliness on to paper? He felt he had nothing to guide him as to that. Faced with an audience, he had the expression on their faces to tell him how he was doing. He felt miserably uncertain of himself as he faced blank paper and dipped his quill in the ink. There was nothing to be done, of course, but to try as every writer must. So he wrote and corrected, tore up his papers in despair and began all over again—but still could not be certain if what he had written was saleable, because he didn't know if it was even any good, and he could not bear the thought of making a fool of himself in public. So he kept his

efforts a secret. When he had at last polished one story
to his liking, he copied it out in his best hand (there
being no typewriters then), and one evening at twi-
light, went out with it and dropped it stealthily
through the letter box of a dark office up a court off
Fleet Street.

He heard nothing of his manuscript for a long
time, but he seems to have been patient. In the end he
stumbled on it in print before any word had reached
him from the editor. He was on his way to the Gallery
and had dropped into a bookshop to see if they had
a copy of the Christmas number of *The New Monthly
Magazine,* to which he had sent his work. The shop
was just closing. He paid his half-crown quickly and
went out down the Strand through the gathering dusk
of a December afternoon towards Whitehall. He did
not look inside the magazine until he had reached
Westminster. Then he found in it *Dinner at Poplar
Walk,* unsigned, but miraculously improved at first
glance by the dignity which print can lend to the
written word.

He was so excited, tears came to his eyes, and he
trembled so he could not face his colleagues immediately in the Gallery.

It is difficult to go back nearly a hundred and
twenty years and see just how the story struck its
first readers. It must certainly have seemed new and
different from anything they were accustomed to.
Probably some of them thought it rather vulgar. The
writing *is* often crude; yet the characters still leap
from the page, and the story has preserved for us
vividly the small detail of the everyday life of the
people.

The story had not been printed under any name

at all, although Charles had provided a *nom de plume*, "Boz." It was a nickname he had given his youngest brother from some joke rising out of the story of Moses in *The Vicar of Wakefield*. Moses, pronounced thickly through the nose, became Botheth, and thence Boz.

Of course he longed to know what his friends thought of the story, and Kolle found a copy of the magazine one day flung down carelessly where he was sure to see it. Through him, Charles knew, the Beadnells would at least know of his small success. Kolle, needless to say, thought it wonderful and was tremendously enthusiastic.

While still waiting to hear the fate of that first effort, Charles had continued writing, and had several more stories ready to try on the same editor. In his eagerness to get a start, he did not make any fuss about not being paid, but immediately dropped six more stories through the same letterbox. All were accepted and, like the first, published anonymously. They appeared monthly from January to May. This was highly gratifying, but a check would have added to his satisfaction. Kolle had a note from him, saying: "I have had a polite and flattering communication from the Monthly people requesting more Sketches, but they are rather backward in coming forward with the needful!"

He never received a penny, as it turned out, for any of these stories. The owner of the magazine was in financial difficulties. Finally, in August, one came out signed "Boz." For a young man who so badly wanted money, the encouragement might have seemed slight, but Charles soon saw that he had been given quite a substantial boost into the writing world. His sketches were being read by people who mattered, and the name of Boz was soon repeated inquiringly among them. He showed the one that was signed to his new editor on *The Morning Chronicle* who, recognizing talent and novelty in the work, commissioned him to write a series on the life of the London streets. Ironically enough, there was to be no extra money for these either. They were to be included as part of his service to the paper, but they carried his name further than *The New Monthly*.

Charles' appointment with the *Chronicle* had started at the beginning of the Parliamentary vacation— a great convenience to him financially. John Black, the editor, was a staunch, large-hearted man to whom Charles took an instant liking. He made friends also with the musical and dramatic critic, George Hogarth, already well known in Scotland, whose fourteen children made the young reporter exuberantly welcome when he visited them.

For the first of the new sketches Charles described London in the early morning, the arrival of produce for Covent Garden Market by wagons, donkey carts and wheelbarrows; the buying and selling there and the porters and the coffee houses; and the coach stations where cold, pale-faced passengers waited for the early coaches amid a babel of hawkers crying penknives, pocket books, small sponges, sets of caricatures and so on.

In the second sketch, he turned to the night life of the little streets where at dusk the muffin man came, his baize-covered tray on his head, swinging his bell, in time for family tea; where, at nine o'clock, the beer man shuffled on his rounds, a lantern fixed to the front of his two-tiered trayload of pots, and where the little grocery shops stayed open until eleven o'clock, their windows throwing pale patches of light before their doors.

In those days people lived more exclusively in their own small sets and, at least in London, the rich had no notion of how the vulgar middle class lived; and the middle class knew nothing of the squalor of life among the very poor. What Charles did was to capture the essential feeling of everyday life, sometimes among one group of people, sometimes among another. He got them hot on to the page so that his readers believed him, or at least found him convincing. Great curiosity developed and the demand for his writing grew.

His first assignment for his new paper took him to Edinburgh to report the speeches at a dinner at which Lord Grey was to be made a Freeman of the City on the occasion of his retiring from the office of Prime Minister. Charles traveled north by boat with his colleague and friend, Tom Beard, and had the pleasure of actually seeing a man roaring with laughter over his latest story, *The Bloomsbury Christening*.

It was part of the reporters' business to get back with their news at the first possible moment—there was as yet neither telegraph nor telephone. On this occasion Charles let *The Times* men beat him by twenty-four hours. This was not at all to "Blasthope's" liking. Success in getting back first depended mainly on what posting arrangements could be made for the return journey. *The Times* men left the hall as soon as the speech they were concerned with was over, at midnight on *Monday* the 15th. They traveled by post-chaise and reached London on *Wednesday* at six in the morning. The printers were ready to set up the type immediately, and copies of the paper were on the

road back to Edinburgh the same evening. By one
o'clock midday on Friday they were on sale there.
Edinburgh to London in thirty hours was good going
and depended on there being no delay over changing
horses throughout the journey.

Charles took this lesson to heart and became a
master of ingenuity in saving minutes by good planning and artful contriving.

The Houses of Parliament were burnt down that
autumn. The story of how it happened was one Dickens
always liked to tell, as illustrating the awful futility of
the red tape of his day.

The Law Courts were then grouped together to the
west of Westminster Hall, and among them was the
Court of Exchequer (Treasury Department). For cen-
turies accounts had been recorded here by the primi-
tive method of making notches in talley sticks. In the
reign of George III it had been proposed to substitute
books for sticks, but it was another fifty years before
the idea was accepted, and the dry, splintering ruler-
like pieces of elmwood were still regarded as "Con-
fidential," since they represented official records and
receipts. They could not be disposed of, therefore,
even for firewood for the poor, but were stacked up
by thousands in store rooms where they occupied
much space and grew drier and more inflammable
every year. At last, in the autumn of 1834, someone
made a bonfire of them in a stove under the House of
Lords. They flared up as though soaked in paraffin
and the flames roared up the chimney. The blaze got
out of control. Wood panelling in the rooms above
began to smoulder, then caught fire. It was soon discovered and the alarm sounded. A detachment of

Guards was instantly dispatched at full speed to put it out. They would probably have done so before much damage had occurred, but that they were stopped on their way by an officer who objected that the regulation number of pioneers were not with them. By the time he was satisfied and the men had been permitted to proceed, the fire had such a hold that both Houses were gutted and the historic chapel of St. Stephens, where the Commons had met since 1547, was completely destroyed.

Charles soon began to hunger again for a place of his own where he could have peace to think and to write, and where, too, he might escape some of his father's incessant borrowing. Letters show him constantly having to borrow for himself small sums to "tide over" till pay day. This was greatly against the grain, and no help to a young man with ambitions. He began to long for a home of his own and thought of a suite of rooms furnished to his fancy in the recently built Furnival's Inn. Once again his father's affairs interfered with his plans. One of the army of creditors lost patience and, though Mr. Dickens with his usual cunning slipped away, he was not clever enough. He went out with his twelve-year-old son, Alfred, ostensibly to try to raise money, but sent the boy home while he hid himself. Knowing "how apt Father is to get out of the way when anything goes wrong," Charles was not worried at that. Mr. Dickens, however, was arrested next day and taken to the "sponging house" in Cursitor Street. Here arrested debtors were lodged temporarily with bailiffs who tried to make them pay up, as one might squeeze a sponge.

Tom Mitton, of Gray's Inn days, was a great help at this time, and Charles wrote him several letters

about his father's position. One asked him to "go over
to Sloman's in Cursitor Street and ascertain whether
anything can be done." Another said, "I must work
this morning, but tell him please that I shall be with
him at six. I fear it is an awkward business and really
I have no idea of the extent of his other embarrass-
ments."

That was the trouble. The debts, though small
individually, were so numerous that Mr. Dickens himself had no idea what the total might amount to. At
any moment, too, one of them might produce a crisis
such as the present one.

This time the family split up, and the business of
supporting it devolved largely on Fanny and Charles.
He had already taken the rooms in Furnival's Inn, but
now moved in with his fourteen-year-old brother,
Frederick. There was no money for even the bare
furnishing, and the "flare" with which he had meant
to celebrate the occasion was out of the question.

It so happened that while he was in that wretched
condition an American journalist arrived to inter-
view the promising young writer known as Boz.
Charles himself opened the door to his ring and stood
there, as the visitor recorded, "in a ragged office coat
buttoned up to the neck." He stood aside for the
stranger to enter and the American looked coolly about
him at the "bleak and uncarpeted room" whose sole
contents he noted as "a deal table, two or three chairs
and a few books: a small boy and—Mr. Dickens."
It was a painful moment and Charles excused himself
awkwardly, dashed into another room and changed
into respectable clothes as rapidly as he could. It was
hard on his return to meet the patronizing eye of his
visitor, who so plainly despised him for his poverty and

told him sharply, "My good fellow, if you were in America with that fine face and ready quill, you would have no need to be condescended to."

Mrs. Dickens loudly and tearfully implored her family to find the money to get her husband clear of the bailiffs, but in vain. John Henry Barrow told her very plainly that he would not put his hand in his pocket again for her or her husband. He took the opportunity, in the bad old, Victorian way, of forbidding either of them ever to cross his threshold again. He thought Charles should have sided with him, for it would have been to his advantage. But, though he had no illusions about his father's weaknesses and extravagances and made no excuses for him, Charles could not go against the family. Instead, he informed his uncle stiffly that doors which were shut against his parents must remain closed also against himself.

First with the News

CHARLES FOUND THE LIFE OF A REPORTER HARD AND exacting whether he was at work in the Gallery, or out on a country assignment. The heavy and controversial program before the House caused Parliament to sit far into the night, and when the members dispersed, the reporters in the Gallery had still the task of transcribing their shorthand notes (unless they had found time to do so between shifts of duty), and getting them to the newspaper offices. The men who were responsible for verbatim reports found the strain on their hearing very heavy, and often suffered from writer's cramp. Though rotating turns gave them some time off, this was sometimes hardly long enough to rest their hands. The next man had always to be in place and taking down before the last stopped writing, for fear of any gap in continuity.

Charles always worked with intense concentration. Not for nothing did Tom Beard speak of him as the "fastest and most accurate man in the Gallery." At the end of a session, he often found himself too wakeful to sleep. He found the night air—the early morning air—refreshing then, and liked to stroll about the streets, watching the dregs of humanity unravel itself from the shadows of night. He stared at sleeping houses, at beggars huddled on doorsteps, at watchmen in their boxes, at the few other men he encountered, all with the same penetrating curiosity. Fear for his safety on those night prowls seems never to have occurred to him, and a love of nocturnal wandering grew with the years, showing him much that other men never dreamed of.

He had become one of the most trusted men on *The Morning Chronicle,* and was chosen to follow Lord John Russell, perhaps the boldest and ablest of the Whig leaders. He traveled all over the country to report Russell's speeches. Fortunately, Charles felt a genuine admiration for him. Party feeling often ran high at his meetings, and there were some wild scenes during election campaigns.

One of his earliest experiences of a country election was early in January when he went to report a by-election at Chelmsford. In a letter to Henry Austin he described how he had "been ordered on a journey. Don't laugh. I am going (alone) in a gig, and to quote the elegant inducement which the proprietors of Hampstead *chays* hold out to Sunday riders, 'the gen'l'm'n drives himself.' I am going into Essex and Suffolk. It strikes me I shall be spilt before I pay a turnpike. I have a presentiment I shall run over an only child before I reach Chelmsford."

He gave further news of his adventures four days later to Tom Beard, writing from the Black Boy Hotel at Chelmsford.

"Owing to the slippery state of the roads on the morning I started, I magnanimously declined the honor of driving myself, and hid my dignity in the inside of a Stage Coach. As the Election here had not commenced, I went on to Colchester. Yesterday I had to start at 8 o'clock for Braintree—a place twelve miles off—and being unable to get a saddle horse, I actually ventured on a gig—and, what is more, I actually did the four and twenty miles without upsetting it.

"I wish you could have seen me, tooling in and out of the banners, drums, conservative emblems, horsemen and go-carts, with which every little green was filled, as the processions were waiting for Sir John Tyrell and Baring. Every time the horse heard a drum, he bounced into the hedge on the left side of the road, and every time I got him out of that, he bounded into the hedge on the right side. When he did go, however, he went along admirably. The road was clear when I returned and with the trifling exception of breaking my whip, I flatter myself I did the whole thing in something like style!"

Many years afterwards Charles recalled another meeting during a by-election in South Devon which he had attended to report Lord John for the *Chronicle*. He took it down somehow in Castle Yard, Exeter, "in the midst of a lively fight by all the vagabonds in that division of the county, and under such pelting rain that two good-natured colleagues who happened to be at leisure held a pocket handkerchief (over his notebook) after the manner of a state canopy in an ecclesiastical procession" to keep it dry.

On all these country assignments, Charles had to remember the lesson learned at Edinburgh, which was to plan the journeys so as to gain for his paper the distinction of being "first with the news." In this he came to excel. He studied maps and learned the roads, became adept at short cuts and knew the ins and outs of every posting inn and stable on the way. Many of his night rides were thrilling and hair-raising.

Charles gave a description of one of them in a letter to Tom Beard.

"I have not the slightest doubt (God willing)" he wrote, "of the success of our express. On our first stage we had very poor horses. At the continuation of the second, *The Times* and I changed horses together. They had the start of two or three minutes. I bribed the post-boys tremendously, and we came in literally neck and neck—the most beautiful sight I ever saw. The next stage, your humble caught them before they had changed (horses)."

The Times man on that occasion had achieved his two minutes' advantage by bribing their post boy to drive into the Inn at Honiton by the back way, which let them get their fresh horses out ahead of the *Chronicle's* chaise, unobserved—but Charles still beat them, all hands down.

"We had a *much* longer account than any other paper," he wrote triumphantly to Beard, "and the whole affair is considered one of complete and signal success! . . . noticed as 'a feat' by *The Spectator* and another Sunday paper.

"I feel the effects of the rain severely," he went on. "I came up by the slow coach, left Wincanton at nine on Saturday evening, and reached town at eleven yesterday (Sunday) morning. I have a slight touch of rheumatism and am perfectly deaf.

"What have you done about my bag? For heaven's sake forward it immediately, for I have not a clean shirt to put on!"

Lord John was defeated on that occasion, but ran again in the following November, and Charles was sent to report him. He had arranged to leave town by the early coach and did not get to bed at all the night before. About five in the morning he was in his rooms in Furnival's Inn, writing a letter which said, "I am writing by candlelight, shivering with cold and choked with smoke. The fire, which has been fed like a furnace at the gas works all night with a view to my early breakfast has turned unaccountably white and dusty at the very moment when it ought to boil a kettle. I *think* it is rather a disagreeable morning, but can't say exactly because it is so foggy. My laundress, who is asthmatic, has dived into a closet—I suppose to prevent her cough annoying me—and is emitting, from behind the door, an interrupted procession of the most unearthly and hollow noises. My portmanteau absolutely refuses to suffer itself to be locked although it has been strapped and buckled and stood upon. . . . And rumors have just reached me that 'there ain't no cabs on the stand!' "

Tom Beard was with him on this trip and they were "working sharply together," on a well-planned campaign. "As all papers have arranged to leave Bristol the moment Russell is down," his note informed the London office, "one of us will go to Marlborough in the chaise with one *Herald* man, and the other remain at Bristol with the other *Herald* man to conclude the account for next day. *The Times* has ordered a chaise-and-four for the whole distance, so there is every prospect of our beating them hollow."

He wrote also to George Hogarth's eldest daughter, with whom he was becoming very friendly, of being "in such a chaotic state of confusion, surrounded by maps, roadbooks, oslers and post-boys, that I have no time to devote to anything but business."

Dickens certainly knew the roads and the inns of old England and had the most intimate acquaintance with every sort of vehicle which plied for hire on the roads in the grand old coaching days. It was an experience he valued, and he told his friend Forster about it in a letter he wrote in 1845.

"There was never anybody connected with a newspaper," he wrote, "who, in the same space of time, had so much express and post-chaise experience as I. And what gentlemen they were to serve in such things at the old *Morning Chronicle!* Great or small, it did not matter. I have had to charge them for half-a-dozen break-downs in half-a-dozen times as many miles. I have had to charge for damage to a great-coat from the drippings of a blazing wax candle in writing through the smallest hours of the night in a swift-flying carriage and pair. I have had to charge for all sorts of breakages fifty times in a journey—without question—such being the ordinary results of the pace at which we went. I have charged for broken hats, broken luggage, broken chaises, broken harness—everything but a broken head which is the only thing they would have grumbled at paying for!

"I have often transcribed for the printer," he went on, "from my shorthand notes, important public speeches in which the strictest accuracy was required—and when a mistake would have been, to a young man, severely compromising—writing on the palm of my hand by the light of a dark lantern in a post-chaise and four, galloping through a wild country and through the dead of night at the then surprising rate of fifteen miles an hour. I verily believe I have been upset in almost every description of vehicle known in this country. I have been in my time belated on miry by-roads towards the small hours, forty or fifty miles from London in a wheel-less carriage, with exhausted horses and drunken post-boys—*and have got back in time for publication*—to be received with never-forgotten compliments from Mr. Black, coming in the broadest Scotch from the broadest heart I ever knew."

He witnessed some disgraceful election scenes in the course of his journalistic work, and wrote to a friend about one of them. "A slight flare here yesterday morning just stopping short of murder and a riot. Party feeling runs so high. I look forward to a scuffle before it is over. As the Tories are the principal party here I am in no very good odor in the town. Would you believe that a large body of horsemen, mounted and armed, who galloped on a defenceless crowd yesterday, striking about them in all directions and protecting a man who cocked a loaded pistol— were *led by a clergyman and magistrates!*"

~~~~~~~~~~~~~~~~~~~~~~~~~~~~~

CHAPTER X

Engaged to Be Married

CHARLES PLODDED ON WITH HIS STORY WRITING ALL THAT
year in whatever time he could snatch from reporting,
though what he earned by it was hardly enough to
provide him with paper and quills. He was tough, and
he had trained himself to ride hard as well as "roughshod." He knew he was getting known, but he still
desperately needed money. So he asked to be paid
when he was invited to write a new series of sketches
for the evening edition of the paper which the owners
of *The Morning Chronicle* were launching. "No great
amount, of course," he added modestly, "but *something.*" There must have been some principle involved
for even then a separate fee for the stories was not
allowed. Instead, his salary was increased by a regular
two guineas ($10) a week, which he found perfectly sat-
isfactory. The sketches were signed and illustrated by
George Cruikshank. The first appeared in the first
number on the evening of January 31, 1836.

George Hogarth was now editor of *The Evening
Chronicle.* He had grown up in Edinburgh where he
was educated for the law, but went into journalism,
instead, shortly after his marriage. Hogarth, after making a name for himself as a music critic, became Secretary of the first Edinburgh Musical Festival. He thus
came into contact with some of the greatest of Scottish

authors and artists, among them Sir Walter Scott. It
was his proud boast that he had been "the friend and
companion of the great Sir Walter." When he became
editor of the new London evening paper, Mr. Hogarth was living in Fulham, at 18 York Place—and a
full, busy house it must have been when all his children
were at home.

The Hogarths were home-loving, hospitable people
who loved visitors. Charles went there often and enjoyed a romp with the small fry almost as much as
the talk with their parents. Soon he also was heard
to boast sometimes of his friend, "Sir Walter's intimate friend and companion." The family atmosphere
was exceedingly pleasant after his treatment at the
Beadnell's and Charles felt very much at home there.
There were several daughters, of whom the eldest,
Catherine, was three years younger than Charles, and
he promptly fell in love with her. Her sister, Mary,
was about fourteen, and Georgina, a mere child of
eight. With all three he had rather special connections
in the course of his life. He married Catherine,
cherished Mary with particular tenderness, and came
to regard Georgina as the prop and mainstay of his
own large household many years later.

It was gratifying to be accepted as a young man
with a future. Charles expanded and relaxed under
the compliment. He had changed in more than a
matter of prospects since the days of his infatuation
with Maria. In these few years he had developed in
mind and personality. He had regained faith in himself, and knew a good deal more of the world, and
of women. Now he did not plunge headlong and
uncontrollably into his affair with Catherine as with
Maria—yet he did not manage it very well either.

Probably he did not understand her and thought he could mold her to his fancy once they were married, hoping to inspire in her, by his own fire, something which he felt to be lacking even quite early in their engagement.

She was small and rather nice looking, but with a weak, small mouth and rather over-large luminous eyes. It was the sort of face which might mature into real beauty; and six years later she was indeed beautiful, if a portrait painted of her at that time by the famous artist Maclise is to be believed. But in character she showed all the prickly archness, affectation, perversity—and stupidity—of so many of the heroines of Dickens' novels. She teased and plagued him, sulked and turned cold, was offended and would not speak, accused him of neglecting her, and required to be constantly and cravenly wooed into good humor.

The letters he wrote to her during their engagement—and he wrote many—give a very clear picture of the relationship between them. He was continually cajoling her, rallying her, reasoning with her, trying to convince her of the simple fact that he *wanted* to be with her every minute of the day and that when his work kept him from her, it was at least as hard for him as for her that he had to work hard for the sake of their future together. She does not seem to have responded to his arguments, though one has to judge of that without much evidence. She kept all Charles' letters and they still exist, but towards the end of his life he made one great bonfire of all the correspondence he had accumulated throughout the years and expressed an earnest wish that everyone who had kept letters of his should do the same. We should have lost much if they had, for his letters are lively and very revealing, telling a great deal (by their style) of his character and temperament, as well as describing his daily life.

As soon as she had her marriage preparations to occupy her, Catherine seemed to become more tractable. Her spirits rose a little as the air became full of glorious excitement about clothes and furnishing.

When the engagement had been but three weeks old, he had written "with the greatest pain" to remonstrate with her for "the display you have favored me with twice already ... the sudden and uncalled for coldness ... such sullen and inflexible obstinacy".... He begged her "if a feeling of you know not what, a capricious restlessness of you can't tell what, and a desire to tease, you don't know why, give rise to it— *overcome it*. It will never make you more amiable, I more fond, or either of us happy.

"I know as well as if I were by your side at this moment," he went on, "that your present impulse on reading this note is one of anger—pride perhaps or, to use a word more current with your sex, *spirit....* My dear girl, if you really love me, I would have you do justice to yourself, and show me that your love for me, like mine for you, is above the ordinary trickery and frivolous absurdity which debases the name and renders it ludicrous. I am *not* angry, but I am HURT."

Catherine certainly did not recognize even dimly the kind of man she was going to marry. Her ambition did not rise beyond the world she knew, and she probably thought of Charles, at best, as settling into some comfortably assured position like her father's, in the course of time. It does not look as though she attached much importance to his other scribbling, and it was the extra time he had to spend on the sketches which she so bitterly grudged. She lacked the spark in herself to recognize genius and hail the unknown future. For her the safe, cosy, humdrum way of life was most to be desired. It was probably this incompatibility of temperament which she expressed so often in her sulky moods.

Nevertheless, to his great satisfaction they became engaged in April. A few weeks later he took temporary lodgings in Selwood Place, near her home, so that they could see more of one another. But he kept on his rooms in Holborn and continued to work there, although he slept generally at Fulham. He found it pleasant, after he had finished with the paper and handed in his reports, to stroll through the City in the very early hours of the morning and, perhaps to drop a note into the Hogarth letterbox as he went by on his way to bed. He had sent his notes formerly by her father or brother, or even occasionally by the hand of his own brother, Frederick. From Selwood Place he often wrote asking her to grace his table at breakfast, to come in and wake him—with Mary as chaperon.

"I hope to be wakened by your tapping at my door in the morning," one of them ran, "and I look forward on making my appearance in the sitting room, to find *you* heading my table."

Charles was enchanted at the prospect of marriage and the transformation of his utilitarian bachelor home into something, as he hoped, fresh and warm and glowing. He could hardly bear the brief time of waiting. He was not in the least afraid of any difficulty in supporting a wife though he knew it might be hard going for a time. He had his newspaper pay and he had just received an outside commission to write a series of twelve sketches for a sporting paper called Bell's *Life of London*. He felt pretty sure more work would come in—possibly more than he could easily deal with in the snatches of time he could command.

He never wrote easily, never to order, but often filled his wastepaper basket with failures before he got into the feeling of what he wanted to do. Then, once his pen had begun to flow, he wrote quickly and to good purpose. As he still did not feel he could trust his judgment, he always feared that he might let rough, unfinished work go out simply because of the pressure under which he had to do it.

Another writer whose books are still read today was tasting the first moments of fame and enjoying it enormously. This was Harrison Ainsworth, whose first historical romance, *Rookwood,* had recently been published and had proved an instant success. He was making important friends and found they were impressed by his comments on the work of less known men. He began to fancy himself as a spotter of talent, and was interested in those unsigned sketches in the old *Monthly Magazine.*

Ainsworth lived at Kensal Lodge, Willesden, then a country village, where he entertained many of the famous men of the literary world, who rode or drove out to visit him. He now invited Charles, who found himself flattered and patronized. He wondered that Charles had not thought of gathering up his sketches and making a book of them, and on the spot, introduced him to his own publisher, John Macrone. Charles had no time to do more than beam with delight when an offer was actually made him.

Macrone was a shrewd judge of a book—that was

well known—but he was apt to drive a hard bargain; that was well known too. When the publisher rose to Ainsworth's airy suggestion, the spotter of talent was delighted at his own cleverness. He knew very well that nothing would have transpired unless it had looked like good business to Macrone. It was an exciting moment. Macrone paralyzed Charles with a bid for outright purchase. He offered a hundred pounds ($500) and the promise of pictures by Cruikshank to make a nice book of the sketches. It was so tempting, so opportune, Charles could not look critically at the price. What could he not do with a hundred pounds at that moment? He knew what an attraction Cruikshank's work would be, how it would recommend the book widely and lend it dignity. He would be proud to see his sketches published in such a style. He accepted without more ado, offering eagerly to make any revisions Mr. Macrone might advise or to write one or two more pieces if that would help. He had one already in mind about Newgate Prison and perhaps another on the House of Correction in Clerkenwell. Mr. Macrone liked and accepted both ideas, and promised to pull a string or two to get Charles inside Newgate.

Charles was quick to avail himself of this help in order to see the dark secrets of Newgate. His eyes were all for the prisoners, though he noted, too, the things which he thought most likely to interest the man in the street, the shackles and irons, the condemned cells, the chapel. He found a great variety of types herded there together, a boy in livery, a man in rough great-coat and top boots, a "desperate-looking fellow in his shirt sleeves with an old Scotch cap on his shaggy head," and he found them all alike in one respect—all seemed "idle and listless." He looked into the prison chapel with the condemned pew, its "most conspicuous object in the confined space, a huge black pen in which the wretched men singled out for death are placed on the Sunday preceding their exe-cution, in sight of all their fellow-prisoners from whom they have been separated but a week before, to hear prayers for their own souls, to join in the responses of their own burial service, and to listen to an address warning their recent companions to take example from their fate."

It was to these scenes that his mind returned when he was writing the last chapters of *Oliver Twist*. They played their part, too, in shaping his conviction that the death sentence was wrong and a crime against humanity.

Catherine and her mother caught scarlet fever towards the end of that summer and Charles, risking the infection, visited her as often as he could. When he could not go in person, he often sent Frederick with a note, a message, or a little present, a pot of black currant jam one day for her throat; chloride of lime on another "to purify the atmosphere."

While she was ill John Dickens found himself in trouble again and, as ever, called on Charles to help him out. It was the same miserable tale all over again of old debts and creditors losing patience.

"The unhappy sketch had only reached its third slip by dinner time," one of his letters to Catherine runs. "Father was worrying here this morning until nearly two o'clock, and after he went I fell asleep, having been so unwell with my side last night as to be obliged to call up Fred."

Anxiety always knocked him out and he struggled

through his strenuous days handicapped by headaches,
stomach upsets and the old spasm. Interviewing creditors on his father's behalf was always a disturbing
business and he wrote to Catherine of an "unpleasant
set-out of yesterday." A week or two later he wrote
begging her not to be angry with him for not coming
in person. "I have only this moment returned from
accompanying Father to Cold Bath Fields, i.e. to the
House of Correction. My sketch is not yet commenced
and Dowling (the editor of Bell's *Life of London*)
tells me that if he has it at all, it must be before
nine o'clock tomorrow morning.... Now, however
strongly disposed to be 'coss' you may feel at first, I
am quite sure you will not continue so long, and that
you cannot fail to see that I have no alternative but
to set to work with what appetite I may. God bless
you, dearest girl.... Love to all, Believe me, Dearest
Pig, Ever yours most truly and affecty. Charles Dickens.
990000000000000 kisses."

The production of his *Sketches* was going ahead
so he had to make time to see Cruikshank about the
illustrations. Dickens was always very particular about
the correctness of detail and scene in pictures to accompany his work, and this makes the original illustrations of special interest.

His way to the artist's house took him through
Pentonville where new streets were being laid out,
and he took the opportunity to inspect some of the
new houses to see if any might suit him and Catherine.
He thought the Pentonville air good and found the
houses "pretty," but thought them "extremely dear at
a rent of £55 ($275) a year with taxes.

He had already given notice at Furnival's Inn that
he would be giving up his present rooms at the end

of the year. He now applied for a larger suite, and resolved to make that the home to which he would bring his wife.

In the middle of all these preoccupations, he was sent out to report more election speeches of Lord John Russell's, and on his return found Macrone asking urgently for the new sketches he had promised. The truth was that he had found it hard to write those two particular scenes and had put them off and off. Now that his own father was in the House of Correction he felt quite unable to make a story about it. He wrote to Macrone excusing himself on the grounds that "the treadmill will not take hold of men's feeling as the gallows do." Macrone agreed to drop that one, but insisted that he must have the Newgate sketch, and soon. So much had happened since Charles' visit that he actually found difficulty "in remembering the place and arranging my material."

"My composition is peculiar," he told Catherine, "I never can write to any effect—especially in the serious way—until I have got my steam up, or in other words until I have become so excited with my subject that I cannot leave off."

~~~~~~~~~~~~~~~~~~~~~~~~~~~~~~~~~~

CHAPTER XI

Pickwick

1836 WAS A BIG YEAR FOR CHARLES. IT WAS A FATEFUL year, remarkable for its opportunities and for his achievement. In it he took a flying leap into the heart of the literary world. He had his first big commission; and out of it came a work which has become one of the immortals, *Pickwick Papers*. He made important new friends, among them Sergeant Talfourd, a very distinguished and charming person who knew everybody and was universally admired and respected. He was a Sergeant at Law (which was the highest degree for a lawyer in Common Law), but his heart was in literature. He delighted in discovering young writers and bringing them to the notice of those who could help them. He counted himself a critic and his taste and judgment were widely deferred to. He was genial, kind, generous; his manners were easy and so gracious that few remained nervous with him long. He was as welcome in the houses of the great and famous as in the dingy rooms of struggling young men.

For a time Talfourd was Law Reporter for *The Times* and, in this connection, first came across Charles. He was elected to Parliament in 1835 and introduced the first Copyright Bill in the House of Commons. It was thrown out, but it had made a stir, and our modern idea of copyright is still largely based on

Talfourd's conception of it. It certainly set Charles thinking. Had he not just sold a copyright for a hundred pounds so that, however successful his book might prove to be, however much money it made for his publishers, he would have no right to another farthing from it?

It was Sergeant Talfourd who introduced Dickens to a woman who was to play an interesting role in his life. She formed a deep friendship with him and spurred him on (in accordance with his own inclination) to use his pen, his observation, humor and common touch to expose the social wrongs and sufferings of the day so as to rouse public interest in reform. This woman was Angela Burdett, daughter of Sir Francis Burdett, M.P. for Westminster, and granddaughter of the founder of Coutts' Bank, whose fortune she inherited at his death in the following year.

She was twenty-one when she first met Charles, grave, lovely, and very much aware of the responsibility the possession of such wealth laid upon her. In her own home she had met and talked with the most distinguished and brilliant men and women of the day. She was accustomed to being taken seriously by them, even as a child. She went deeply into matters that interested her, and was particularly concerned with the problems of how to relieve suffering and distress especially that caused by poverty and neglect.

This was the ground on which she and Charles met so warmly. He was right, she told him, to want to do good with his gifts. What he laid bare in his writing, she must try to remedy with her money. They must, they would, help each other. Angela Burdett came to rely on him for her facts. When she wanted to know what conditions were like in prisons, workhouses, the lowest of lodging houses, for instance, it was to him she turned. When she saw a chance to help in a good cause, such as Lord Shaftesbury's "Ragged" Schools, it was again to Charles that she looked for the facts which no one else could give her, facts which were more than statistics and took account of the humanity and endurance of even the most wretched and degraded man and woman. It was his insight and understanding she valued, his quick eye and warm heart. She spent enormous sums of money on good works and became as great a public figure, it was said, as Queen Victoria herself.

At first her earnestness seems to have subdued Charles, though it was not long before his natural high spirits burst through again. He wrote merrily of their first meeting, that "it must have been on a Friday, for I was born on a Friday and never began a book or began anything of interest to me or of importance but it was on a Friday!"

Talfourd took him also to Holland House, a trying ordeal, for Lady Holland always expected her lions to roar. Carlyle met him there for the first time about four years later and wrote of the occasion, "I did see lords and lions, Lord Holland and Lady, Pickwick, too, though they do not seem to heed him over-much. He is a fine little fellow, Boz, I think. Clear blue, intelligent eyes, eyebrows that he arches amazingly, large protrusive, rather loose mouth, a face of most extreme mobility which he shuttles about, eyebrows, eyes, mouth and all, in a very singular manner while speaking. Surmount this with a loose coil of common-colored hair and set it on a small compact figure, very small and dressed *à la D'Orsay* rather than well—this is Pickwick. For the rest, a quiet, shrewd-looking little fellow who seems to guess pretty well what he is and what others are."

On Charles' twenty-fourth birthday, *Sketches by Boz* was published, and he sent copies with graceful little notes wherever he thought they might do the book some good. One went to Lord Stanley, one to Harrison Ainsworth; one, of course, to Talfourd. As the publication date drew near Charles worried about publicity, and the appearance of advertisements and puffs in the papers. He had intended to write something to push it in the *Chronicle* but when the moment arrived, found the idea of praising it himself so distasteful that only a bare announcement appeared there. The book was, in fact, well reviewed and highly praised in many dailies and in the literary periodicals. John Forster reviewed it in *The Examiner,* and this led to their meeting.

Forster was a North-country man, a couple of months younger than Charles, immensely capable, active and tireless. He was a lawyer, and brought a lawyer's clear grasp of essentials to the task of dealing with author's and publisher' business. He had a forthright manner like a businessman's, and was accustomed to speak his mind. He took Charles to his heart, gave him good advice, discussed his work and talked over his plans with him, corrected his proofs and, in fact, made himself best friend and right-hand man.

This was the moment at which the proposal came which resulted in Charles Dickens writing *Pickwick Papers.* The publishing firm of Chapman and Hall—which also had the bookshop in the Strand from which Charles had bought that copy of *The Monthly Magazine* in which his first writing had appeared—wanted

an amusing text to go with a series of pictures proposed
by an artist, Robert Seymour, whose work they had
already produced with some success. They considered
various other young writers before the name of Boz
came up. This writer of the popular sketches seemed
more promising than the rest, and Mr. William Hall
called on him in person to broach the idea. It was a
coincidence, and seemed to Charles a good omen,
that it was actually from the same gentleman that he
had bought the famous copy of the magazine. Charles
recognized him as soon as he saw him again.

Mr. Hall, looking into that restless, eager face
which Forster described as "beaming wonderfully with
intellect and running over with humor and cheerful-
ness," explained the outline of the proposal he had
come to make. Would Mr. Dickens care to write a
short text for pictures to be supplied by their artist,
describing the supposed proceedings of a sporting club
to be called the *Nimrod Club* whose unskilful members would embark on a round of hunting, shooting
and fishing expeditions in cheerful ignorance of the
elements of sportsmanship?

Charles listened thoughtfully and with mixed feelings. It was flattering and very exciting to be sought
out for work. Goodness knows he wanted any money
it might bring him badly enough, with his marriage
approaching—not to mention his father's everlasting
peccadilloes—but could he make a hit with a job like
this? He felt uncomfortably that he did not know
enough of sport to be amusing about it. (As it is, the
pages of *Pickwick* rather suggest that he knew more
about sliding on frozen ponds than he did about
cricket!) He did not think it would be a good thing

to undertake a commission, however tempting, unless he felt he could fulfill it with credit to himself.

He explained ruefully what was in his mind and wondered, with his intelligent eyes on the publisher, whether in fact the idea was so bright and new after all. The *Jorrocks* books were just coming out and wasn't there just the slightest suggestion of imitation in the Nimrod Club? Besides, he thought it all upside down for a text to be written for pictures. It was more natural for the writer to provide the ideas and the artist to illustrate them—in any case he did not think he could write in that way. He would have to have a free hand to create his own characters; he preferred to choose his scene and invent the action.

Mr. Hall appreciated the point of view. He had been sizing him up and now said he thought he could arrange matters to suit him. He then went into the business details of the proposal, that he wanted to issue monthly parts at a shilling (twenty-five cents) a time, each containing twenty-four pages of text and four full-page drawings. For the author's part they were prepared to pay fourteen pounds ten shillings ($72.50) per installment.

Charles asked for time to think it over and Mr. Hall gave him two days. He accepted, of course.

Mr. Hall warned him then that the publishers would always want to have more than one installment in hand before they went to press, in order to avoid the risk of a breakdown. Charles quite understood that danger, and set to work at once, wondering how he was going to fit in the extra writing, but determined to manage it somehow. "The work will be no joke," he told Catherine cheerfully, "but the emolument is too tempting to resist."

Compared with at least one famous writer of the period, Dickens was now doing very well indeed. Thomas Carlyle, a man of probably greater intellectual power and with aspirations as great as Charles' own, industrious and conscientious, had come to London to earn his living as a writer two years before. He brought with him a total capital of a little over two hundred pounds to keep him and his wife until he could get a footing in the literary world. Just as Charles was coming to his decision about *Pickwick*, Carlyle wrote in his Journal, "The first book of *The French Revolution* is finished. It is now three-and-twenty months since I earned one penny by the craft of literature ... but, thanks to thrift and my Scotch wife, we can hold out many months yet."

The extra work proved to be, as Charles had said, "no joke." His letters to Catherine reveal how hard pressed he soon became—and how engrossed in his new task. "You must not be 'coss' with what I cannot help," said one. "I like the matter of what I have done today very much but the quantity is not sufficient to justify my coming out tonight. If the representations I have so often made to you about my working as a duty and not as a pleasure be not sufficient to keep you in good humor—why then, my dear, you must be out of temper, and there is no help for it.

"I can fancy, if you began to read this note with a frown, that a smile has taken its place by this time, so I shall speak rationally about what I have been doing as I hope I shall always be able to do to my own wife. I have got Pickwick and his friends on the Rochester coach, and they are going on swimmingly, in company with a very different character from any

I have yet described, who I flatter myself will make a decided hit."

This character was Jingle. His "indescribable air of jaunty impudence and perfect self-possession," his little tricks to avoid paying, strongly suggest that he was based on John Dickens. Certainly the style of talking, the jerky breaking off after every few words was characteristic of Mr. Dickens. For instance, "Commodore? My coach—place booked—leave you to pay for the brandy and water—want change of a fiver!" A throaty cough makes the interruptions, "Any luggage? Who—I?—Brown paper parcel here, that's all—other luggage gone by water—packing cases, nailed up—big as houses—heavy, damned heavy." The type of anecdote again was John Dickens'—"Heads! Take care of your heads! Terrible place—five children—mother—tall lady, eating sandwiches—forgot the arch—crash—knock —children look round—mother's head off—sandwich in her hand—no mouth to put it in—head of a family off—shocking, shocking!"

(This sad accident to a lady, by the way, was supposed to have been based on an incident which occurred when a coach was drawing out of the Golden Cross Inn yard at Charing Cross.)

It is quite interesting at this point to take a look at a copy of *Pickwick* and try to see how the first and subsequent installments shaped up and what went into each. Jingle makes his appearance within the first dozen pages, so Charles had still a long way to go when he wrote to Catherine about the new character on March 6th—and the first number was to be published before the month was out. In the first chapter Charles obviously found it heavy going to introduce all his Club members and get them clearly identified.

The last cab on the stand

As soon as that was done, how happily he let himself
go on one of the London scenes he knew so well from
personal experience, just the kind of episode he used
so successfully in his sketches. Times without number he had himself gone down to the coach stand in
St. Martins-le-Grand, just as Pickwick did—the stand
where coaches had already stood for more than three
hundred years. Cabs stood now alongside the coaches,
and how well Dickens knew the cabbies with their
sackcloth coats and aprons, their brass number plates,
and the rude saltiness of their Cockney wit!

So, in a very short time Charles had his little party
packed into the *Commodore* and on the way to Rochester—his beloved Rochester where he had known such
happiness as a child. He had never been back to it
since that day, thirteen years ago, when he left it,
"packed like a parcel" for London. You can feel his
spirits rise, as he recalls the scene, and the writing runs more easily as he describes the Bull Inn,
still standing much as it was then, so that you can,
if you are lucky, even sleep in the same room which
Mr. Pickwick occupied at the end of his journey. He
chuckles over the ways of Chatham worthies, using
Jingle as his mouthpiece. "Dockyard people of upper
rank don't know Dockyard people of lower rank—Dockyard people of lower rank don't know small gentry—
small gentry don't know tradespeople—Commissioner
don't know anybody!" Had Charles heard that from
his father or noticed it with his own eyes as a small
boy? Who can say?

He was delighted with his beginning, and wrote
"in Pickwickian haste" to Mr. Hall, "Pickwick is at
length begun in all his might and glory." He ended
the first installment in good shape, though the second

emerged heavily when it came, as though having only worked on short pieces he found it unexpectedly difficult to continue in the same light spirit. He only just managed to deliver the manuscript for the second installment before the first appeared.

Pickwick came out as *The Posthumous Papers of the Pickwick Club, containing a Faithful Record of the Perambulations, Perils, Travels, Adventures and Sporting Transactions of the Corresponding Members. Edited by "Boz." With four illustrations by Seymour.* It was bound in green paper with a design showing Mr. Pickwick asleep in a punt, his fishing rod over the side, and birds pecking at his neglected lunch.

Only four hundred copies were bound as a start—and no more were needed. Strange as it seems to us, *Pickwick* was not an immediate success.

~~~~~~

CHAPTER XII

A Growing Reputation

THROUGHOUT THE MONTH OF MARCH, CHARLES WAS working hard on *Pickwick* in every moment he could spare. "The sheets are a weary length," he moaned to Catherine. "I had no idea there was so much in them." They made his eyes and head ache, and inspiration simply would not come. "I think the weather makes me stupid," he wrote again. "I've been poring over my desk the whole day and have only perpetrated ten slips—in other words, only one fifth of the whole article."

He and Catherine were to be married soon, and he was, therefore, also occupied in making his new set of rooms in Furnival's Inn fit to bring his wife to. He always enjoyed planning his homes, and had quite a flair for furnishing. His letters are full of references to his purchases—"I have bespoken Mother to come and buy linen. I am very glad your Mama is pleased with the report of the kitchen"—"As your Mama has not seen the sideboard, and as there are a great number of purchases which even *you* have not seen (!) I think the best way will be for you and she and Mary to spend the day here on Saturday . . . ."—"I have bought a pair of quart decanters, and a pair of pints, a crystal jug, and three brown dittoes with plated tops for beer and hot water, a pair of lustres and two *magnificent* china jugs—all I flatter myself slight bargains."

The wedding was to be on April 2nd, at St. Luke's, Chelsea, "and it strikes me," he wrote, "that the best plan would be, when we are married, for us to go straight to Rochester. Mother can write to the Old Lady's servant, and she, I have no doubt, will procure us comfortable lodgings there."

Catherine's moodiness still disturbed him, and he continually implored her not to yield to ill-humor, calling her coaxingly his "dearest Pig" or "old lady" —which sounds very odd coming from the days of William IV.

Tom Beard was best man at the wedding, and described it as "altogether a very quiet piece of business. The only persons present beyond the members of the Dickens and Hogarth families were Macrone, the publisher, and myself." Henry Burnett (later to be Fanny's husband), when asked years afterwards what he could remember of the occasion, had little more to add for, he explained, "Mr. Dickens had not yet taken hold as he did soon after. A few common, pleasant things were said, healths drunk, and all seemed happy.... She was a bright, pleasant bride, dressed in the simplest, neatest manner."

As Charles had suggested, they went then to Rochester and stayed for a week at Chalk, on the Rochester-Gravesend road.

The first number of *Pickwick* had come out three days before his marriage, and the publishers paid him for the first two installments before he left town. He had seen that the second was ready for the printers, except for the fourth illustration, which was to be of the clown's death for *The Stroller's Tale*. He and Sey-

mour, the artist, were not working together well enough
for Charles to feel easy about the engraving being
made in his absence. As soon as he returned, he made
a point of going to see it. He found it quite out of
keeping with his feeling for the scene, and trouble
quickly arose about it.

Seymour had never liked having his original idea
upset to suit young Boz, and there is no doubt that
he was difficult to work with. He felt Charles' writing
did not give him enough scope for his style of work
and he resented criticism, especially as Dickens' objections were sometimes supported by the publishers.
Seymour, for instance, had originally made Mr. Pickwick long and lean while Charles insisted that he
should and must be rotund. Charles won. Mr. Hall
pointed to a family friend as just the figure that was
needed and from whom, in fact, the well-known picture of Pickwick was drawn. It hurt Seymour's pride
to have to revise his work in that way and he met
the criticism of his drawing of the clown's death with
sullen antagonism.

Mr. Hall begged the two men to try to come to a
better understanding, and Charles invited Seymour to
his rooms to talk it over. The drawing was produced
and Charles very civilly explained his views, but the
atmosphere remained cold and the artist resentful.
Seymour spent the next day fiddling moodily with
the drawing; and in the afternoon he went out into
the garden at the back of his house and shot himself.

It was a terrible shock to everyone, and might well
have been the end of *Pickwick*. However, the second
installment was allowed to appear, bearing a notice
giving the "melancholy news of the death of Mr. Seymour under circumstances of a very distressing na-

*Sam Weller in the yard of the White Hart Inn. His appearance
brought success to* Pickwick Papers

ture." Then a frantic search began for another artist.

Thackeray, in the name of Michael Angelo Tit-mouse, applied but his humor hardly suited the author's. R. W. Buss, father of the founder of the North London Collegiate School for Girls, also offered his services. Two of his pictures were actually used for the third installment, but he was not thought good enough to continue the series.

Then out of the blue came a young man, barely twenty, who caught the spirit of *Pickwick* so exactly that, without more ado, he was commissioned to take on Seymour's job. He was Hablot Browne and as *Phiz* to Dickens' *Boz* became the perfect collaborator, the inspired illustrator of a great man of the famous novels.

Charles breathed a sigh of relief when that matter was settled, but the publishers had other worries, for *Pickwick* was not catching on as they had hoped. Booksellers reported no eager rush for copies and reviewers paid it little attention. There had as yet been no formal agreement between Charles and his publishers and the firm now felt obliged to ask him to agree to changes in their original terms. They thought it wise to increase the amount of text in each issue from twenty-six pages to thirty-two and at the same time to pay less for them. Charles accepted a reduction of four pounds ($20) a month with what grace he could. Mr. Hall promised that the fee would be increased, if circumstances warranted it. There were also to be only two illustrations instead of four. Charles was to find, all in good time, that his publishers could be generous when the position changed for the better.

When it appeared in book form, Charles wrote a Preface in which he tried to explain some of the disadvantages of writing in installments when each part had to be sufficiently complete in itself to attract new readers, yet keeping a thread of suspense strong enough to lead on to the next issue. It suffered, undoubtedly, through being written piecemeal, with much improvisation when the public's attention showed signs of flagging, and too little thought for the plot as a whole and the broad outline of scene and action.

Charles was rarely more than one month ahead of publication, and what he set down in haste he must often have repented at leisure; but once in print it had to stand. He could never go back and revise early chapters, no matter how character or plot developed later on. He learned by experience and, with all its failings, *Pickwick* still holds a high place, not only in English literature, but almost all over the world. Pickwick, the Wellers and Jingle are still by-words, and their quips caught on quickly as they came from Charles' pen.

His friends told him it was "a low, cheap form of publication," more likely to ruin his hopes than to make a name for him. Stories published in monthly parts had no recognized place in the literature of the time. Such as there were, were trash, interminable tales carried round the country by peddlers as Charles knew, for he had "shed innumerable tears" over them, he said, before serving his "apprenticeship to life."

It was in the fourth installment that Sam Weller made his first appearance—and the sales sped swiftly up to 40,000 copies a month on his waggish backchat. Almost at once the publishers, true to their promise, increased the author's fee and it became twenty-five guineas ($125) a month.

In *Pickwick* Charles found his first chance to let

fly at the law. His treatment of the action for breach
of promise brought against Pickwick himself was so
lightly handled that he gained the readers' sympathy
without seeming to ask for it. Only a dozen years
afterwards, he was able to say, "Legal reforms have
pared the claws of Messrs. Dodson and Fogg, and a
spirit of self-respect, education and cooperation has
diffused itself among their clerks ... the laws relating
to imprisonment for debt are altered and the Fleet
prison is pulled down. Who knows," he added, "but
it may yet be discovered that even Poor Laws may
have mercy on the weak, the aged and unfortunate;
that Schools on the broad principle of Christianity
are the best adornment for this civilized land; that
Prison doors should be barred on the *outside* no less
heavily and carefully than they are barred *within;*
and that the universal diffusion of common means of
decency and health is as much the right of the poorest
of the poor as it is indispensable to the safety of the
rich and of the State."

Meanwhile, Catherine was feeling her way in her
new life. The small flat of three rooms may have
seemed cramped after her family home, and no doubt
she missed the company of brothers and sisters during
the long hours when Charles was out at the House of
Commons or working at his desk at home. Frederick
was living with them and made some sort of company for her in the evenings, but it was certainly not
an ideal life for her.

Frederick was not much like his brother. He had no
thirst for education, no perseverance and very little
ambition beyond the desire to have money to spend.
Already he was finding it distinctly pleasant to be
known as Charles' young brother and he liked carry-

ing letters to Charles' interesting friends. During that summer, a post (which he did not keep very long) was obtained for him at Mr. Macrone's offices, in the counting house, and Charles, asking that he should be allowed to come home for tea each day, explained that he liked to see Frederick before he went out in the evening—"to set his studies and to see what he is at."

Though Charles' life may have looked delightfully easy and profitable to the young brother, those were in fact critical days: much depended on how he fulfilled the promise of his earlier work. He had as yet no security whatsoever and with his mercurial temperament he must have wavered wildly between high expectations and apprehension of disaster. He was working wastefully, destroying thousands of words written for every piece he thought fit to be used, yet he was aware of the growing strength of his powers. But for the sort of work he was doing freshness counted, and he grudged more and more the long hours in the Gallery, yet he dared not give up the regular job.

He was earning a fair income, between reporting and writing, but with so many calls on his purse he never felt easy about money. It seemed to him that this anxiety had prevented his striking a good enough bargain for his work and he began to nurse the least little bit of a grievance about it. He suspected that other people were making more than their fair share. He had no one to guide him in these matters and he knew very little about the publishing world. He was in a terrible hurry to succeed and had very little notion what he could do about it.

John Dickens had been released from the House of

Correction and was back at Bentinck Street before his son's wedding, but none the wiser for his incarceration. He went on borrowing and giving I.O.U.'s wherever he could. Of course, he had no thought of paying off existing debts. He had grown a good deal more artful and knew the ropes so well that in general he expected to keep clear of positive unpleasantness. He understood to a nicety just the moment when disappearance was advisable, and when the cloud might be said to have blown over. From each he returned to his family as rosily exuberant as ever.

But someone had to take care of the bills, and there were only Charles and Fanny to do it. None of Mrs. Dickens' family would bestow another penny on them. No doubt the Barrows' attitude was fairly expressed by Mrs. Micawber in *David Copperfield* when she said, "my individual impression is that the gulf between my family and Mr. Micawber may be traced to an apprehension on the part of my family that Mr. Micawber would require pecuniary accommodation. I cannot help thinking that there are members of my family who have been apprehensive that Mr. Micawber would solicit their names (I do not mean to be conferred in Baptism on our children) but to be inscribed on bills of exchange, and negotiated in the money market."

Charles was always a good son to his parents and they took advantage of the fact. Probably no one was watching his progress more keenly and with more self-interest than his father. He must have rubbed his hands together gleefully, recognizing that there was a fair prospect of something extraordinarily promising turning up soon, as he heard the respectful terms in which young Boz's future was spoken of. His nimble mind discovered new avenues to explore, new rays of conjuring money out of other people's pockets—a man to man approach to some of his son's new friends, or a carelessly dignified request for the loan of a week's rent, say from his publishers. Very soon he made the enchanting discovery that there were people who would pay—yes, actually pay good money—for Charles' autograph, or a scrap of paper rescued from his wastepaper basket.

Charles endured all these things—not without remonstrance—until he was forced to the conclusion that his father must be got out of temptation's way if that were humanly possible, but for two more years he bore with him.

Charles Dickens' reputation was indeed growing so rapidly that other people were also casting calculating glances in his direction. He had already the look of becoming a money maker, and he was young, eager and ambitious. He should go far. In May, Mr. Macrone made him an offer for another novel and Charles signed the contract a month later, agreeing to write and deliver it in six months' time for double the price he had been paid for the *Sketches*. The price looked inviting when he put his name to the papers.

A couple of months later a Mr. Richard Bentley, who had plans to publish a new magazine, invited him to become editor for a fee of twenty pounds ($100) a month, with which was coupled the offer of five hundred pounds ($2,500) for a story to run serially in it. The task of editing was not expected to be onerous and the magazine was not likely to materialize before the following January. But both these offers for stories were *outright* payments, and were tempting indeed. Charles accepted both.

He would hardly have been human if he had not begun to do some rare pieces of arithmetic, totting up his fabulous-sounding earnings and calculating future prospects, setting them against his spendings and dreaming of heavy savings, security, and freedom at last to let his imagination work for him. He could count on forty-five pounds ($225) a month from his writing alone, with two stories commissioned ahead in addition to *Pickwick*—and still he had to spend long precious hours every night in the Gallery for a mere seven guineas ($35) a week, and with a weekly sketch thrown in at that!

It happened that a particularly scurrilous case was brought into Court that summer against Lord Melbourne, the Prime Minister, and Charles was sent to report it. Sensational developments were expected but it appeared to be simply a gigantic and disgusting piece of blackmail. The plaintiff had expected to be bought off, had never dreamed he would have to substantiate his accusations in a Court of Law. He had no case and his witnesses were worthless. The whole business stank in the nostrils of decent people, and Charles returned from Court raging at the waste of his time.

"I am tired to death," he wrote to Macrone, "*Melbourne vs Norton* has played the devil with me!"

"I devoutly hope ere next session," he wrote to another friend, "I may make some other arrangement which will render its (Parliament's) sittings *a matter of indifference to me,* as the storybooks say, *forever afterwards.*"

He had, in fact, done with reporting, though he

could not quite make up his mind to say so at once. It had yielded him a fair living and had given him some good friends. It had brought him in contact with some useful people and had given him an acquaintance with matters of the moment which was of the greatest value to him, and which he could not easily have obtained in any other way.

~~~~~~

CHAPTER XIII

Oliver Twist

THE OLD SOCIABLE SATURDAY NIGHTS AT THE DICKENS',
when Fanny's musical friends dropped in and there
was music and singing, charades and endless talk,
had led to the airing of several ambitions. Charles had
pursued his love of the drama. John Hullah had been
inspired to set down on paper some of the tunes that
were always ringing in his head. Between them they
had worked out some ideas about stagecraft, production and performance. Out of all the talk and experi-
menting grew a little operetta called *The Village Coquettes*, words by Charles, music by Hullah.

They produced it at Furnival's Inn before a few
friends. The performance went well and when it ended
Mr. Macrone, who was one of the small audience, came
forward with one of his snap offers to buy the copyright. This time, elated though he was, Charles hesitated. He had become suspicious of this way of doing
business and, also, he had Hullah to consider. Finally
he refused and Hullah sold his score independently
to a music publisher for what he considered a pretty
good price. It was an exciting outcome of their enterprise, but more was to follow.

Charles took a month's holiday in the early autumn. He rented a furnished cottage at Petersham,
near Richmond—a strangely beautiful and untouched

oasis even today. To Charles and Catherine it was a country holiday in the fresh air, with the river, fields and woods to tempt them out of doors, yet near enough to town for visitors. Macrone came to see them with some idea still of the little operetta, and brought with him the manager of the recently built St. James's Theater. When they returned to town the script of *The Village Coquettes* went with them. It was accepted for immediate production, and the stage manager won Charles' heart by the brief message, "It's a sure card! Bet you ten pounds ($50) it runs fifty nights!"

Charles had also shown Macrone and his friend that day another trifle which he and Hullah had done together, one of his sketches which he had turned into a farce during his honeymoon, calling it *The Strange Gentleman*. This, too, was taken for consideration, was liked, and went into rehearsal immediately for production before *The Village Coquettes*.

It was amazing luck! Charles went back to Furnival's Inn walking on air, with two works actually to appear at a London theater! Moreover, the first printing of *Sketches* was sold out and another in preparation, and a second volume had been asked for. It was all tremendously exciting, though there was a worm hidden in the rose petals. This early reprint of his book confirmed all his misgivings about the folly of outright sales. If the run continued, and of course he hoped it would, other people would reap a nice harvest at his expense. He was buying experience, but had not yet learned his lesson, for he signed away another copyright almost immediately to Macrone. It was for a novel, named in the contract as *Gabriel Vardon, The Locksmith of London,* though it came to be known as *Barnaby Rudge.*

Charles had still said nothing at the office about giving up work in the Gallery after the vacation, and he drew his pay right through that summer. It was only after he had made a new agreement for sketches to run in both morning and evening editions of the paper that he actually sent in his resignation. And then he felt distinctly aggrieved to find his editor displeased.

Catherine was expecting a baby in January, and her sister Mary now came to stay with them, to be company for her. Presumably Frederick went elsewhere, for the three rooms would have been a tight squeeze for all four of them.

Mary was sixteen, sensible and unspoiled, gay, sympathetic and, fortunately, quite free from the moods and odd humors which marred Catherine's character and made her so difficult to live with. The sisters were good friends and got along well with each other. Mary thought Charles wonderful and gave him a simple, honest admiration which he found quite delightful. She succeeded in supplying the something which turned the suite of rooms into a home, a place of warmth and happiness and sparkling gaiety.

As Catherine could no longer go about with him, Charles took Mary to the theater, to parties, to his publishers, and found that his friends liked her very much. He saw that appreciative eyes followed her wherever she went and that he was complimented on her looks, her wittiness, her good sense. She was a success as Catherine had never been, but the attentions she received did not spoil her. She was good for Catherine, and induced a new sweetness in her as they sat together, sewing or knitting for the baby.

During this time Charles was a great deal at the

theater. *The Strange Gentleman* had opened at the St. James on Michaelmas Day. It was to be succeeded immediately by the operetta, and on December 6th a grand gala performance was given which included both items.

A month later Catherine presented him with a son, and Charles' cup seemed full. That it should have happened on his favorite festival, Twelfth Night, gave him special pleasure. He was in the highest spirits, and he and Mary went romping down Holborn, hand in hand, to find a low nursing chair for Catherine. He announced the birth, drank the health of the young Charles Culliford Boz, planned the christening—which had to be postponed and postponed and postponed yet again—and began to look for a larger home where there could be rather more distance between his desk and the baby's cradle.

In March still another of his works was put on at the St. James—a comedy called *Is She His Wife?* All three received poor notices from the critics, but for Charles it was seventh heaven just to be part of the theater, to have a place at rehearsals, a voice in the production. He never tired of attending performances, and sent tickets most generously to his friends and acquaintances. Indeed, he wasted a good deal of time on the theater one way or another during that six months, but he did not lose his head. He recognized that he had not written a masterpiece in any of these trifles. At the end of their run, he never wanted to see any of them revived. They were the exuberant experiments of a very young man, and it would not have been human for him not to have revelled in the experience while it lasted.

He was prevented from neglecting his bread and

butter during this period by the constant reminders from printer or publisher that installments were due, and that Bentley was expecting from him the first number of the *Miscellany*. It was to contain the first part of a new story by him, *Oliver Twist, the Parish Boy's Progress*. The idea came to him partly out of what he had heard in the House of Commons, and partly from the stories the little orphan had told him when he was a boy. She had been brought up in that institution at Chatham where he made Oliver first see the light of day. For the pictures of Fagin's den of thieves and the tangle of slums where they passed their time, he drew much on what he had seen with his own eyes.

It was always rare for Charles to be at a loss for a character. He had such a multitude of memories to draw upon. All were as alive as when he had first seen the originals and with their past as well as their present so often written for him in their features. But, when it came to the magistrate before whom Oliver was hailed, he deliberated on a model with particular care. He already knew the reputation of the man he wanted to use, but was anxious to watch him at work, so as to get the authentic note of his voice. He therefore asked a friend to smuggle him into Court one morning on some pretext when Mr. Laing was sitting on the Bench at Hatton Gardens. Laing was a harsh man, given to fits of ungovernable rage. It is significant that not long after the publication of those scenes in *Oliver Twist*, the Home Secretary thought it wise to remove him from his post.

We may find the innocence and gentle manners of Oliver when the parish had done with him quite unconvincing. Charles, however, was only expressing a conviction which had grown out of his own experience, that strange qualities seem to be born in children in the most unlikely environments. Though it was incredible to readers of his day, he was right in feeling that no one is doomed to a life of degradation because of a misfortune of birth and parentage. He knew the minds of the people he most wanted to reach. Perhaps he judged them by the level of intelligence and responsiveness he found in his own parents. He felt sure he could not hope to rouse their interest without playing heavily on their feelings.

Reading was a novel form of entertainment for the public he aimed at. They knew little of life outside their own immediate circle of friends and neighbors. They were far from intellectual and very easily moved to laughter or tears. Charles knew how to please them and how to rack them, but he had a serious purpose in almost all that he undertook. It seemed to him that they must be told how other people lived. He had seen measures for reform become Acts of Parliament, but was persuaded that laws could not change life unless ordinary people understood what was behind them and made their own personal efforts to change conditions.

He was often reproached for writing about such shocking characters as Bill Sikes and his Nancy, Fagin and the Artful Dodger—no one seems to have questioned his Oliver! When the book went into its third edition some years later, Charles replied to these critics in a special preface.

"I have read of thieves by scores," he wrote, "seductive fellows, amiable for the most part, faultless in dress, choice in horseflesh, bold in bearing, fortunate in gallantry, great in song, a bottle, a pack of cards or dice box; fit companions for the bravest. It appeared to me that to draw a knot of such associates in crime as really do exist, to paint them in all their deformity, in all their wretchedness, in all the squalid poverty of their lives; to show them as they really are, forever skulking uneasily through the dirtiest paths of life, with the great, black, ghastly gallows closing up their prospect, would be to attempt something that was greatly needed, and which would be a service to society. Therefore I did it as I best could.

"In every book I know, where such characters are treated of at all, certain allurements and fascinations are thrown around them. Even in *The Beggars' Opera,* the thieves are represented as leading a life which is rather to be envied than otherwise.

"What manner of life is it which is described (in *Oliver Twist*) as the everyday existence of a thief? What charms has it for the young and ill-disposed, what allurement for the most jolter-headed of juveniles? Here are no canterings upon moonlit heaths, no merry-makings in the snuggest of all possible taverns, none of the attractions of dress, no embroidery, no lace, no jack-boots, no crimson coats and ruffles, none of the dash and freedom with which *The Road* has been, time out of mind, invested. The cold, wet, shelterless midnight streets of London, the foul and frowsy dens where vice is closely packed and lacks the room to turn, the haunts of hunger and disease, the shabby rags that scarcely hold together: where are the attractions of these things?

"No, as the stern and plain truth was a part of the purpose of this book, I will not abate one hole in the Dodger's coat, or one scrap of a curlpaper in the girl's dishevelled hair. I have no faith in the delicacy which cannot bear to look upon them."

Charles had been writing *Pickwick* and *Oliver* alternately, turning from one to the other as the next installment of each fell due. It had been hard going in the close quarters of Furnival's Inn, with the baby crying a good deal and the fires always spread about with small garments, airing. At last, however, he found a house which was convenient and within his means. It was in Doughty Street, and is now preserved as Dickens' House, the home of the Dickens' Fellowship. Doughty Street is broad and the houses on either side are pleasant places. In those days the road was closed at either end with gates in the care of watchmen in livery. Mary Hogarth remained there with her sister, and Frederick rejoined the household. Two servants and a boy were engaged. With no telephone, a boy to carry messages was a necessity for such a busy young man as Charles.

The move was safely accomplished and Charles breathed again. The magazine was proving a great success and making a good deal of money for Mr. Bentley. It brought Charles credit and he did not find the editing arduous. *Oliver* was being well received and Charles still felt adequately paid by the five hundred pounds he had received. Now, however, Bentley asked for a second story to follow *Oliver*, and on the same terms; and for another after that, also on the same terms. He must have hoped to make hay while the sun shone, but he had opened his mouth too wide. Charles revolted.

~~~~~~

CHAPTER XIV

Forster to the Rescue

THE EXCITING DAYS OF 1836 ENDED, THOUGH THE TIDE of success lapped over into 1837. In April, the first anniversary of *Pickwick* was celebrated at a banquet with compliments showered on the smiling author. A month later the very fabric of his life seemed torn apart, for Mary died suddenly, and literally in Charles' arms.

It was on a Saturday night, and they, with Catherine and the Dickens parents, had been to the theater. The three returned to Doughty Street in high spirits, supped gaily and went to bed. Before he was out of his clothes, Charles heard a sound and went out on to the landing to listen, crossed to Mary's door and knocked. When he put his head inside, he found her gasping for breath. Catherine came at his call of alarm, but she had never seen an illness like it before. Frederick ran for the doctor but when he came he could do nothing, and had no idea of the cause.

Mary struggled painfully through the night, Charles supporting her as she lay on the bed and coaxing brandy into her mouth from time to time—but all to no purpose. In the early afternoon he watched her die —little more than twelve hours after she had been laughing and joking with him and Catherine.

Mrs. Hogarth reached the house just before the

end, collapsed and had to be put to bed there. Charles was distraught, and found himself with the dismal business of making the funeral arrangements. Mary was buried at Kensal Green, and on the headstone, he wrote: "Young, beautiful and good: God numbered her among his angels at the early age of seventeen."

After the funeral Charles could not face the house with all its memories. He took Catherine away to stay for a few weeks at an ancient timbered farmhouse at Hampstead, a place where, before them, artists and a poet had found inspiration. William Blake had placed the little garden looking towards the Spaniards, and had stood "in tranquil reverie" before the low door looking out to the wooded slope. Along the front of the house ran (and still stands) a verandah with a light roof through which the strong, stalwart trunk of a great cherry tree has grown. It was here that Charles and Catherine used to sit, watching the spring turn to summer over the low hills to the north.

Friends came out to sympathize and stayed to talk of Mary, Macrone among them, and Harrison Ainsworth, Maclise the painter, and John Forster, eager to help in any way he could. He listened feelingly and there laid the foundation of their long and lasting friendship. He came away feeling himself entirely in Charles' confidence, as intimate as though they had known one another all their lives. At the end of a month Charles felt able to write again and was ready to face the blankness of his home.

He came back to work with a different perspective and looked with distaste on all the contracts to which he had committed himself. The prospect now appalled him. How could he possibly fulfill them? How could he get out of them? But there was Forster at

hand, kind, capable, knowing. With his legal training
and strong, forthright character he seemed a blessed
friend in need. Charles lost no time in confiding to
him the whole confused story. Forster had already
made up his mind that Boz was a young writer worth
watching and helping. He listened gravely and pa-
tiently to the end, asked for facts and documents and
promised to examine the position and see what could
be done. Charles had to admit that he had not always
bothered about documents, had not even kept copies
of the agreements he had signed so blithely and now
regretted so bitterly.

It was not easy to get back into harness after the
upset of the past weeks. Charles groaned over the
thousands of words of *Pickwick* and *Oliver* required
of him each month, and sighed for inspiration as he
tackled the extra contribution now demanded by the
Miscellany. He saw that Macrone was advertising
Gabriel Vardon as "forthcoming"— and not a word of it
written! Then there were Bentley's two contracts, the
first with a date drawing uncomfortably near. Well
might he have cried with the Psalmist, "My enemies
hem me in on every side, on every side I say they
hem me in!"

He was in an impossible position and felt driven
beyond all bearing. It is hardly surprising that he
resented having to write a story for Macrone for two
hundred pounds ($1,000), when Bentley would pay
him five hundred ($2,500). He longed to get rid of
Macrone's contract, and asked Forster to see if that
was possible.

Harrison Ainsworth was extremely conscious that
Charles had owed to him that first offer of Macrone's
which had so gratified the young writer at the time.

John Forster

He was watching him now from a distance and guessing pretty shrewdly what was going on. Charles' success had ruffled him a little. He envied him the editorship of Bentley's *Miscellany*, so he felt no qualms about dropping a word in Macrone's ear, advising him to stand on his rights and to call in his lawyer if need be.

Macrone, always peppery over money matters, was much harassed at that moment about the state of his business. He took Ainsworth's tip, and dug in his heels when Forster approached him. Their talks hung fire and Charles grew frantic for fear he would be obliged to hold to his bargain after all. In desperation he cut across Forster's polite negotiations and tried his own hand. He actually succeeded in getting back the contract for *Gabriel Vardon*. With Bentley, Forster was more successful, persuading him to drop the second of his two contracts and to postpone the date for the delivery of the first. At that Charles breathed again, and proposed to fulfill the Bentley contract with *Gabriel Vardon* under the title of *Barnaby Rudge*.

This wretched state of affairs had arisen partly from Charles' natural anxiety to make money quickly, and partly because of the extraordinary speed with which he had risen in the literary world. He was becoming a best seller absolutely without parallel in the experience of the publishers of his day. His market value soared so wildly, almost from month to month, that an offer which seemed quite generous when it was made already had a mean look even a few weeks afterwards. By the time he was ready to fulfill it, the gilt was off the gingerbread altogether—and Charles could never forget that he was the creator of the thing the publishers sold. He never wrote easily, was never expert enough technically to "toss off a book."

The imaginative effort of creating characters and devising plots and situations literally wrung the sweat from his brow. He had a tremendous vitality which enabled him to work at high pressure for long periods, but he did so to the ultimate ruin of his health. After barren hours at his desk, he sat up late too often grappling with a confusion of ideas which would not fall into the pictures he wanted to paint. The strain made him restless so that, instead of going to bed, he wore himself out walking about the streets, as he had done in his reporting days.

No sooner had Forster settled the Bentley contracts than a further complication arose—Macrone was planning to re-issue *Sketches by Boz* in monthly installments as nearly like those of *Pickwick* as possible, even to a similar green cover. *Pickwick* had become so popular that everyone, from porters in the markets to judges in the Courts, looked forward to publication day and Sam Weller's latest wisecrack. There would be nothing new in the *Sketches*. All had been published before, some even twice. Charles was frantic. The public would be disappointed, *Pickwick's* sales might be damaged and the reputation of the author tarnished.

Macrone must be stopped. Charles implored Forster to do something and, though Forster had failed before, he was a good go-between, cool and diplomatic, accustomed to considering the other man's point of view while never losing sight of his object. He could be abominably stubborn and blunt, but his integrity was widely respected. He liked to play his fish in his own way, though that often seemed to Charles too quiet and leisurely. Now he went to Macrone and began to probe the situation. The publisher was surly and declared flatly that he had bought the sketches outright and would do what he liked with them. Forster digested this quietly, watching Macrone narrowly. Then he shot at him, point blank, "What would you take for the copyright?" (Macrone had paid one hundred pounds ($500) for it, remember.)

"Not a penny less than two thousand ($10,000)," came the sharp reply.

Forster, scandalized, bade him good day. He advised Charles to do nothing for the moment, to put the matter out of his head: but this Charles could not do. He had worked himself into a fever about it. On the spur of the moment he went to Chapman and Hall and laid the position before them. They paid Macrone his fancy price and bought the copyright, making an arrangement by which Charles should be responsible for part of the purchase money. In the long run even that transaction showed a profit, though Forster always declared that he was "glad he had been no party to a price so monstrous."

That summer Charles made his first trip across the Channel, taking Hablot Browne, his artist, as well as Catherine. They traveled by post chaise from Calais through France and Belgium. Then, towards the end of August, they spent a gay holiday at Broadstairs where Charles romped like a schoolboy on the quaint old pier and the pleasant beaches, playing practical jokes in a way quite beneath the dignity of a rising young author. He rode on donkeys over the green clifftops and forgot how much he had suffered that year.

Pickwick came to a triumphant conclusion in the autumn with "a capital dinner, capital wine and capital speeches" in its honor. Before Charles set out to it, a check for seven hundred and fifty pounds ($3,750) was put into his hands by his publishers. As he rose to propose the toast of the evening, the head waiter set before him "a glittering temple of confectionery, beneath the canopy of which stood a little figure of Mr. Pickwick himself." All his friends were present including, of course, Forster, to whom he had just written, "Your notices make me very grateful, but very *proud*, so have a care of them!"

How circumstances had changed since that momentous day when Mr. Hall had called on him at Furnival's Inn with that first proposition! In those eighteen months Charles had learned something about writing, as a comparison of the early and later chapters shows. *Pickwick* had brought him fame and a good deal of money. Pickwick and Sam Weller, the creatures of his imagination, were already household words up and down the country. No one of any judgment could feel any reasonable doubt that Charles Dickens had a notable future before him.

Hablot Browne had his success, too. His illustrations of the Dickens' novels, some of which have been used to illustrate this book, have preserved delightfully some of the detail of the everyday life of the last coaching days, with the galleried inns, the coachmen, porters, cabbies, the rich and the poor, the life in town and country—and not least, of the lawyers and their offices.

Pickwick done, Charles' thoughts leapt forward to its successor, for naturally the firm which had given him his first chance wanted to have more of his work. He had in mind for them a story of the "cheap" boarding schools then to be found mainly in Yorkshire. The idea gripped him as that for *Gabriel Vardon* had

never done, and he longed to turn his back on Bentley's contract so that he could give himself up to it.
He had no possible excuse, however, for not carrying out his agreement—until Bentley himself provided
a loophole of escape.

It appeared that Bentley had commissioned a
journalist to write up the memoirs of Grimaldi, the famous clown—the same whom Charles had seen with
James Lamert at Drury Lane so many years before.
The manuscript proved unsatisfactory when it was
delivered and Bentley wondered whether Dickens
might care to try his hand at pulling it together. The
account was based on the clown's own words and
Charles had a certain curiosity about the life of such a
man. He read it through but, in spite of some good
stories, felt it was very poor stuff. He agreed to revise
it and to write a preface. He was delighted to find
how clearly he could recall every moment of the performance he had witnessed as a child, and felt that
the memory would help him with the task. He thought,
also, of an easy way of doing it. He employed his
father as stenographer, to take down his dictation
while he smoothed out the language as he went along,
making it flow under his tongue.

John Dickens was delighted and perhaps saw a
pleasant future for himself as his son's secretary. But
it was a lazy way to do the job and did not prove
very successful; nevertheless it brought Charles a fee
of three hundred pounds ($1,500) and, when he handed
Bentley the manuscript, he persuaded him to extend
the time fixed for the delivery of *Gabriel Vardon*. That
settled, he found himself free to work on the book he
really wanted to write next, and that was *Nicholas
Nickleby*.

~~~~~~

CHAPTER XV

The Yorkshire Schools

DICKENS NEITHER INVENTED NOR EXAGGERATED HIS PIC-
ture of Dotheboys Hall. It was well known that such
places existed. They were advertised frequently in the
London newspapers, and in such a way as to make it
clear that there was an easy way to get rid of un-
wanted children. Charles had known about the "cheap"
schools ever since Chatham days when he had seen a
boy come back from one with a shockingly festered
ear. He may have heard more from his parents, may
even have thought of them in those miserable days in
Bayham Street when, as he wrote later, he would have
given *anything*, just to be sent to school *anywhere*.
His interest started from that time, but had been
rekindled by recent reports of a particularly bad case
where boys had died of neglect. Such items of news
got about slowly then. People were only beginning to
realize that they had power in their hands to stop
abuses, but public indignation had been stirred, and
was rising.

An exposure of these schools was to be the theme
of his new book, but first he had to collect his evidence. He may well have read this as he searched the
advertisement columns of the papers:

EDUCATION—at Earby Hall near Greta-bridge,

Yorkshire, YOUTH are BOARDED, CLOTHED, provided with Books and EDUCATED by Mr. Simpson, in whatever their future prospects may require, at 20 guineas per annum—there are no extras nor vacations. Prospectuses, with references, may be had at the Saracen's Head, Snow-hill, where Mr. S. attends daily, between the hours of twelve and two o'clock, for a few days.

It was at the Saracen's Head, Snow Hill that Mr. Squeers attended daily. Now to Greta Bridge went Charles and Hablot Browne in search of the material they needed. They travelled under false names, for it occurred to Charles that his reputation as author of the topical sketches of London life might prove a hindrance to his present quest. He provided himself, also, with a reasonable pretext for the visit, a fiction about a widowed friend who wanted to find a school in those parts for her young son. He took with him a letter from a London attorney introducing him to another in the market town of Barnard Castle.

They set out at the end of January and as they went north the snow grew deeper. They left the coach at Greta Bridge, where he wrote to Catherine that "about eight o'clock (at night) the snow began to fall heavily and as we crossed the wild heaths hereabout, there was no vestige of a track. The mail kept on well, however, and at eleven we reached a bare place with a house standing alone in the midst of a dreary moor." The place was in utter darkness and the two men watched the coach drive away in a state of acute misery. No one came out to greet them. It was fearfully cold with no sign of life anywhere. To their great joy, however, they discovered a warm wel-

144 THE STORY OF CHARLES DICKENS

come behind the closed doors and barred shutters.
A comfortable room with "a most blazing fire" waited
for them. In half an hour a smoking supper was set
before them and they retired after it to "capital bed-
rooms in each of which there was a rousing fire half
way up the chimney!"

Next morning, after a regular Yorkshire breakfast
which offered "toasts, cakes, a Yorkshire pie, a piece
of beef about the size and much the shape of my
portmanteau, tea, coffee, ham and eggs," they set out
to explore further afield. Only a mile or two ahead
lay Barnard Castle, which was to be their headquarters.

They soon learned that the village of Bowes, four
miles away, was notorious for its schools. There, after
four miles along a high, exposed road over which the
iciest of winds blew, they found the one Charles took
for the scene of Dotheboys Hall. Bowes is still a small
village, straggling along either side of a single street
for perhaps the length of a mile, but in it Charles found
no fewer than four of these sinister establishments. He
tramped up and down the snowy road, past the old inn
and the church in whose graveyard many of those
unfortunate children lay buried, as the register shows to
this day. Seething with indignation he and Browne returned to Barnard Castle and sought out the lawyer to
whom Charles had obtained his introduction.

This man proved to be a big, bluff fellow who, all
unaware, contributed something to the book that was
brewing, in the portrait of John Browdie (who was so
delighted at the news that Nicholas had "beatten the
Schoolmeaster.") As they talked, Charles found that,
whenever he brought in the question of schools for his
friend's little boy, the attorney's broad, jolly face

changed. After a struggle to be discreet, he at last
spoke his mind.

"We've been very pleasant together," he observed
gravely, "and I'll speak my mind t'thee. Dinnot let the
widow send her boy to one of our schoolmasters *while
there is a horse to hold in all London or a gutter to
sleep in.*" He stared hard into the young man's face and
repeated the words with heavy emphasis.

That was all the guidance Charles needed. He inter-
viewed several of the masters who had advertised their
schools, was shown premises and saw with his own
eyes both the leers of the masters and the misery of
their victims. He saw the man he drew as Squeers. The
portrait was apt enough for the original to identify
himself with it and attempt a protest that Charles was
ruining his business.

Before he left Barnard Castle, Charles was sitting
over his coffee one morning in the King's Head Inn,
looking idly across the wide cobbled market place, when
his eye rested on a clockmaker's shop on the far side
with the name of Master Humphrey over its door. He
strolled over, and poked his head inside, noticed the
old-fashioned interior as the sort of scene he might one
day make use of. In fact, he described it as the setting
for his Editor's Chair when he started the magazine he
called *Master Humphrey's Clock.*

All the way back to London, the new story was
shaping in Charles' head. Yet when he reached his
desk, the words would not come as he wanted them.
He wrestled with the description of the place for days.
Then he began his chapter, instead, with an account of
the Nicklebys, but "*I have begun!*" he wrote triumphantly to Forster. "What is more, I can go on." The
first chapter was written in two days, the whole in-

stallment took two weeks. He took it with him one night to read to Forster in Lincoln's Inn Fields, watching its effect on his friend as he read, discussing how it should continue.

Forster had become Charles' most devoted friend and they saw one another almost daily through the next few years. He shared Charles' confidence, and was always ready to drop his own work to listen, advise, criticize—or to join him on one of the walks or rides which provided the relaxation so necessary after long hours of intense concentration. Forster kept most of Charles' letters and they are preserved in the Victoria & Albert Museum. They are curiously revealing. Some, especially in the early days when Charles was still a little in awe of him, have the appearance of copies, they are so neat and careful. Others could only have been written in the heat of the moment, the sense of achievement bursts out of them, the quill splutters, the downstrokes are swelled with energy and confidence. Sometimes again, the hand appears weak and wavering as from near-exhaustion. They took the place of the telephoning of today, and, incidentally, have preserved for us something peculiarly personal and characteristic.

Many of the notes were brief. "What a brilliant morning for a walk!" or "Is it possible that you can't, oughtn't, shouldn't, mustn't, won't be tempted this gorgeous day?" or, "I start precisely—precisely mind—at half past one. Come, come, *come* and walk in the green lanes. You will work the better for it all the week. COME! I shall expect you." Or, again, "You don't feel disposed, do you, to muffle yourself up and start off with me for a good brisk walk over Hampstead Heath? I knows a good 'ouse where we can have a red-hot chop for dinner, and a glass of good wine." Another,

"Not knowing whether my head was off or on (it became so addled with work) I have gone riding the old road, and should be truly delighted to meet you or be overtaken by you."—"Where shall it be—*oh where?* —Hampstead, Greenwich, Windsor? WHERE?????— while the day is bright, not when it has dwindled away to nothing!" One said only, "A hard trot of three hours?!" And another—"to be heard of at Eel-pie House, Twickenham."

In March, 1838, Charles and Catherine had a daughter and called her after their dear sister, Mary Hogarth. Soon afterwards they all went down to Richmond for fresh air. They were still there when the first number of *Nickleby* was published. Charles had been on his honeymoon when *Pickwick* first appeared, and out of town for the first number of *Oliver Twist*, so now he began to build up a legend that he was *always* out of town when his stories were first published. It was only a piece of nonsense, but it gave him opportunities for the gayest of celebrations.

Nickleby proved an immense success. It sold as many at the start as *Pickwick* did of its closing installments. Everyone was delighted.

The young family took a house at Twickenham that summer and revelled in entertaining. There were all sorts of jokes with the children, including a balloon club of which Forster was President on condition that he supplied the balloons; but a vote of censure was recorded "for gross negligence in discharge of that duty," by the whole of the "Gammon Aeronautical Association for the Encouragement of Science and the Consumption of Spirits." Charley was eighteen months old and toddling about. He was now known as "the Snodgering Blee." Baby Mary received the nickname of

the "Popem Jee"—which may have had some connection
with the card game of Pope Joan.

Fanny and Letitia Dickens were married that summer, one to Henry Burnett and the other to Henry
Austin, an architect and surveyor.

Though it was a holiday Charles was putting in a
good deal of work. He had *Oliver Twist* and *Nicholas
Nickleby* on his hands and the stories obsessed him
equally. Nicholas and Smike, Fagin, the Artful Dodger
and Bill Sikes occupied his mind and were his daily
companions. The stories developed more easily on
that account, but were no less exhausting.

"I worked pretty well last night," he wrote to Forster, "very well indeed—but although I did eleven slips
before half past twelve, I have four to write to close the
chapter, and as I foolishly left them till this morning, I
have the steam to get up afresh." And later, "I got to
the sixteenth slip last night and shall try hard to get to
the thirtieth before I go to bed." Another letter showed
how *Oliver* was drawing to a close. "Hard at work still.
Nancy is no more. I showed what I had done to Kate
who was in an unspeakable state—from which I augur
well! When I have sent Sikes to the devil, I must have
your opinion."

He was back in town before *Oliver* was finished.
The end of the story worried him. "No, no, don't, don't
let's ride tomorrow, not having yet disposed of the
Jew," he wrote to Forster. "He is such an out-and -
outer that I don't know what to make of him."

He was sometimes reproached for having drawn
Fagin as a Jew. So, some years later, in *Our Mutual
Friend*, he described, by the way of compensation, a
good Jew such as he knew among his personal friends.
At the same time, he would not admit that there was

much justice in the complaint. He felt he had simply drawn a bad character of the period from his own observations and, as he used to point out, Fagin was, after all, the *only* Jew in that gang of evil spirits.

One of the curious effects of writing as Dickens did for serial publication was the amount of correspondence which reached him about the characters before even Charles himself knew what their fate would be. Eminent public men wrote begging him to deal kindly with Fagin's boys, or with Smike; later to "spare" little Nell or Paul Dombey. Sergeant Talfourd, one evening in Forster's rooms, pleaded for Charley Bates and the Artful Dodger as eloquently as ever counsel for the defense pleaded at the bar for a client's life.

Now, when Charles was ready to set down on paper the end of *Oliver Twist*, he sent round to ask Forster to come and sit with him, to have a chop and to "read, work or do something"—but to be at hand with his sympathetic presence.

"How well I remember that evening," Forster wrote in his *Life of Dickens*, "and our talk of what should be the fate of Charley Bates!"

When the serialization of *Oliver Twist* came to an end in Bentley's *Miscellany*, Charles resigned from the editor's chair. Harrison Ainsworth at once took his place. The magazine had sold well, largely on account of the interest Charles' story had created, and he had again the wretched feeling that other people profited too much from his work. "It was always Bentley's *Miscellany*, never mine," he complained, seeing that the profits of the growing sales went into the one pocket only. *Barnaby Rudge* should have succeeded *Oliver* immediately, but still Charles could not bring himself to tackle it. It hung fire for another year and then the contract was eventually torn up when Chapman and Hall bought the copyright of *Oliver Twist* from Bentley.

Nickleby continued to go well. It was full of lively and memorable scenes, ranging from the Yorkshire school to a peep behind the scenes with a theatrical touring company; from the inside of a high-class dressmaker's establishment to the shady business career of Ralph Nickleby. It is full of great characters, Newman Noggs, the Mantalinis, the Crummleses, the Kenwigses, the Cheeryble brothers—and, of course, Mrs. Nickleby, modelled again on his mother and presenting quite delightfully the foolishness and the obstinacies of a type of elderly lady he very well understood. Yet, though he enjoyed the richness of his own creation, he still found himself always behind with the writing, always with "the printers at his heels," as Forster said.

It will be remembered that Sergeant Talfourd's copyright bill had been thrown out, and authors were suffering very badly for lack of proper protection of their work. Before *Nickleby* was more than a third written, it had been pirated. The dialogue was hacked up, an ending invented and it appeared as a play at the Adelphi Theater. In a state of justifiable indignation Charles went to see it. With an honesty that was characteristic of him, he found himself obliged to praise some things in it. He felt, for instance, that the actors had caught the intention of his characterization well. Nevertheless, it was robbery and infuriating. A plagiarized version of *Oliver Twist* was also appearing at the Surrey Theater. It was so frightful that when its rightful author went to see it he could not bear to watch the horrible travesty of his scenes, but lay down in his box so that he need see no more.

There was also piracy of books going on in America, from which country Charles had been offered a "bonus" on a publisher's profits on *Pickwick* and *Oliver* before he had finished writing them. He refused to be given a present of money which he felt he had a legal right to. He expressed his willingness to make an agreement with the American firm authorizing them to publish his books, but this was rejected. As there was no copyright agreement between the two countries, such an arrangement would not have safeguarded either Charles or the American publishers. Any other firm could still have produced and sold the books at will.

CHAPTER XVI

The Death of Little Nell

CHARLES WAS FAST MAKING HIS NAME. PEOPLE WANTED to know him, and found they liked him as much as they did his books. It was not only his lively mind, his intelligence and gaiety: there was also something unmistakably genuine about him. He could be ambitious without becoming self-absorbed. He was excellent company, loved good talk and had wide interests. He had a great curiosity about the new scientific ideas of the day, heredity and mesmerism, as well as that lifelong addiction to the stage and his unique knowledge of social conditions. Most people enjoyed his rollicking parties. No one could tell a story so well and his vitality was infectious. It is true his vehemence sometimes inspired antagonism, but one by one the disapproving faces yielded to his spell.

Catherine's reactions to this phase of their life were very different. She wanted only a quiet corner where she could be left alone. It was an ordeal for her to play hostess for him on such a scale, and it gave her no pleasure. She was beautiful for the moment, as Maclise's portrait of 1842 showed, but a listlessness was growing on her. More and more she performed passively what was required of her. Decisions she left to Charles, even as to what she should wear, how their house should be run, and about the bringing up of the children, to whom she was not warmly devoted. It seemed that she had little to give them, but Charles luckily made up for her deficiencies. Naturally conscientious, he tried to give his children what he himself had missed, both in upbringing and education. He trained them in his own way to orderliness, and maintained the discipline which he considered as necessary to a good home life as fun and gaiety.

Watching his brothers grow up with their father's weaknesses unchecked had made him reflective. He often wondered how he had escaped their faults. He might so easily have fallen into the same idle ways. He determined, if he could, to make his own children independent and self-reliant.

Trouble was brewing again for John Dickens, and was so serious that he hardly dared show his face out of doors. Charles went to Forster and Tom Beard (his father's friend as well as his own) for advice. They realized that he must act boldly and at once, and suggested the removal of "the prodigal parent" to a cottage in the country away from the temptations of London life. Forster added that only when his father was securely installed there should any attempt be made to deal with the matter of his debts. It was essential that no hint of this plan should be allowed to get out, for fear of any of the seething army of creditors taking steps to prevent it.

Charles, therefore, set out for Devonshire without further delay, leaving his friends to watch over his parents. They were to be dispatched as soon as Charles sent word that a house was ready for them.

At Exeter he found just what he wanted, "a jewel

Catherine Dickens, 1842

(*After a portrait by Daniel Maclise, R.A.*)

of a place," as he wrote to Catherine. "I walked straight
to it this morning. Something guided me, for I went
on without turning right or left and was no more
surprised when I came upon it and saw the signs up,
than if I had passed it every day for years!"

"Now," he went on, "*if* my mother *can*—I don't
urge it if she objects—make up her mind to come down
to me by the *Telegraph* on Thursday morning, I shall
be saved not only a world of uneasiness, but a good
deal of money, for people *will* take me in and I can't
help it. I send a check for the amount of her traveling
expenses, and that little matter of the spoons which I
had forgotten"—(*The spoons!* Is this an echo of Mrs.
Micawber and the pawning of the teaspoons?)—"The
fare inside is three pounds ($15). She must eat and drink
whenever and wherever the coach stops for the purpose. It goes from the Black Bear, Piccadilly, just
beyond the Burlington Arcade."

Mrs. Dickens was not particularly pleased at being
thus shifted away from her friends. But she went down
to Exeter as requested and was very crotchety with
Charles as he showed her the fruits of his labor. Mr.
Dickens joined her shortly after, breezily triumphant at
having dodged his creditors so successfully, and it was
not long before they were grumbling and sending
Charles "sneering, hateful letters."

Forster's cautious probing soon showed a state of
affairs even worse than was feared. It was plain that,
unless his own interests were safeguarded, Charles
might find himself responsible for such a load of debt
as might have made a far richer man blanch. On
Forster's advice he put a notice in the papers dis-
claiming liability for any debts but those contracted
by himself or his wife.

It looked as though John Dickens must, for his own safety, stay out of London and Charles began to hope that he had "settled the governor for life." But this was not so. "The governor" disliked being under any kind of restraint, and was adept at slipping away. He was heard of in Manchester, Birmingham and elsewhere. He thought of wild plans (which rarely matured) such as transferring his establishment to France for the sake of his younger children's education; and he still managed to run up debts which he hopefully looked to his son to settle.

Charles and Catherine went back to Petersham that summer, taking Elm Lodge, a large, beautiful house where they could entertain generously, as he liked to do. While he was there he worked out an idea for a magazine of a more popular kind than Bentley's *Miscellany*.

He wanted it to have a popular appeal, as though he were talking to his friends from a favorite seat in the chimney corner, and these were the seat and the chimney corner he had seen in Master Humphrey's shop that day at Barnard Castle. Chapman and Hall liked the idea and agreed to back it. It was to be called *Master Humphrey's Clock,* and to cost threepence a week.

Seventy thousand copies were sold of the first number, which came out in April, 1840, but when it was found that Boz had no story in it, the sales dropped. They continued to fall until, in the fourth number, *The Old Curiosity Shop* made its first appearance. The story grew out of a tale he had been told once of a child left alone in the world, wise in a young and thoughtful way, who throughout many strange adventures had kept her natural goodness and integrity. The character of the child became identified in his imagination with memories of Mary Hogarth, "so young, so beautiful, so good," and he set her in a background of "wild grotesque characters" so that her goodness would stand out of itself. He made her wander the country over with her aged grandfather, earning a few pennies for bread as opportunity offered, mixing with showmen at fairs, helping to re-dress Mrs. Jarley's waxworks by the wayside; and at last, dying—"Dear, gentle, patient, noble Nell was dead."

The tale swept England, and America as well. Carlyle wept over it. Daniel O'Connor declared that he was nearly out of his mind with grief over her death. Bret Harte told how miners round their camp fires in California followed the serial breathlessly, and that crowds gathered on the dock for the arrival of the boat bringing the latest installment from England, shouting impatiently: "Is little Nell dead?" Lord Jeffery, the famous Edinburgh critic, pronounced Little Nell the finest thing since Shakespeare's Cordelia! In spite of all the pleas to spare her, she had to die in the story so that Charles could offer a last service to Mary. It had shocked him to find how instantly on her death the girl they had loved became something frightening even to her own sisters, so that they shrank from touching her. He hoped to oust that common fear of death by his picture of Nell, "all suffering gone, past all help, or need of it."

As always, Charles suffered greatly in writing these scenes. His letters speak of his concern over "my poor child," meaning Nell, as he had earlier grieved over Oliver Twist as "my poor boy." He rose from writing the chapter containing her death "nearly dead with work and grief for the loss of my child. All night I have been pursued by her, and this morning I am unrefreshed and miserable. I don't know what to do with myself."

In October, 1839, their third child had been born. It was another girl, called Catherine Macready after her mother and Macready, the great actor, who had become one of Charles' very dear friends. This made the Doughty Street house feel small and cramped and Charles decided on a move. He found something much larger and grander at 1 Devonshire Terrace, Marylebone Road, while he was on his way to look at one of the fine houses facing Regents Park, where Macready lived.

The Dickens' elder daughter, Mamey, described the garret room she shared with Katey in a delightfully intimate picture of life in that house in a book, *Father as I Remember Him*. When they were still quite little girls they were expected to keep their room tidy and were encouraged to make it pretty in their own way. Their father inspected every room in the house regularly, but when they had something special to show him, they used to lie in wait and pounce on him as soon as he emerged from his study. They would drag him upstairs and demand his verdict on the new treasure—perhaps a picture they had cut out of an Annual and stuck on the wall with pins. He always praised them if it was neatly done and looked effective, and his cheery, "Excellent! Quite slap-up!" was sweet in their ears.

It was during 1840 that Charles first met Thomas Carlyle and read his *French Revolution*. He found himself warmly in sympathy with the philosophy of "the Sage." He, too, wanted to prod the common people out of their apathy, to show them how much the remedy for their wrongs lay in their own hands. He remembered dull listless faces at election meetings when matters closely concerning them had been under discussion. He carried Carlyle's book about with him for weeks and read it over and over again. It added fuel to his own fire and set moving ideas which were to become, in the course of years, the basis of two more stories—*Hard Times* and *A Tale of Two Cities.*

He was called to act as juryman in August at an inquest on a child alleged to have been killed by its mother. Accustomed as he was to piecing together snippets of fact and fitting them into a background based on his own understanding of human nature, he came quickly to the conclusion that there had been no murderous intention. He took up the woman's case and was successful in getting the charge reduced to one of concealment of birth. He arranged for extra care for her in prison and for counsel to be retained in her defense when she came up for trial at the Old Bailey. Telling Forster about his experience in the Coroner's Court he described how "the poor desolate creature dropped on her knees before us in protestation that we were right."

Charles never made his own concerns an excuse for not bothering about people less fortunate. His whole correspondence, even in the busiest times of his life, shows the unfailing care and thought which he bestowed on each of the many appeals that were made to him for help. He wrote every one with his own hand and the letters have a personal note, as though he meant every word of them.

He wrote so much about poor people and sordid scenes, not because he knew them best, but in order to show the comfortable half of the world what it was really like to live in grinding poverty and in the stinking slums out of which vice and crime came as inevitably as maggots on tainted meat. He wrote of the things he saw with his own eyes and heard as he walked the London streets. He knew the warm hearts of the poor as well as the callousness of the purse-proud. That was not Victorian sentimentality, but plain truth. He had first discovered the tenderness under-lying many a rough exterior from Bob Fagin in the old blacking factory days. It was a lesson he did not admit to immediately, because of his own sufferings at that time, but it ground its way into his consciousness and he never forgot it—poor, ragged, dirty, hungry Bob has his own share of immortality in Dickens' story!

As *The Old Curiosity Shop* drew to a close in *Master Humphrey's Clock,* Charles made up his mind to follow it with the story which had become such a bugbear to him. *Barnaby Rudge* was at last to be written! It had hung fire for so long that he had lost interest in it. It entailed a good deal of research which he found tiresome and, indeed, boring. He had to look up the historical background in the British Museum, where he ploughed through many contemporary re-cords of the Gordon Riots in search of detail which would be authentic and might lend freshness to the tale. These riots, in 1780, were led by a religious fa-natic, Lord George Gordon. They were an attempt to force the government to repeal laws which gave Roman Catholics the same civil rights as Protestants. Over three hundred people were killed in them before they were stopped. But this was not the "real life" that he enjoyed describing. It was not the "real life" to which he had referred when he said that he never cared greatly for criticism of his work as literature so long as he could feel that he had "got real life hot on the page."

He put into the story an account of a raven drawn from experiences with a bird of his own, the first of a long succession of pets, each called Grip. This one, Grip I, died halfway through the story after a stolen meal of white paint. It was doctored with castor oil, which it took with relish and even revived sufficiently to peck several times quite viciously at the hand which was feeding it. Then it took a turn or two up and down the table on which it was being cared for, moving with curious caution. Suddenly it reeled, seemed to hesitate, shook its head "as though in astonished remonstrance," croaked out, "Hallo old girl!" and fell dead.

~~~~~~~~~~~~~~~~~~~~~~~~~~~~~~~~~~~~~

CHAPTER XVII

"The Inimitable" in America

CHARLES HAD NOW WRITTEN FOUR NOVELS, EACH MORE than seven times as long as this book. Throughout the last four years he had had always two and sometimes three stories on hand simultaneously. He was overworked and grew restless, impatient of the everlasting race to be ready for the printer, a race he never won by more than the skin of his teeth. As he thought of ways of escape, he may have remembered a remedy for Mr. Pickwick's troubles which he had put into Tony Weller's mouth, to "have a passage taken to 'Merriker, and then let him come back and write a book about the 'Merrikans as'll pay his expenses and more." That, at least, is what he now resolved to do, and if he had an opportunity there to explain how he felt about the lack of copyright protection, so much the better.

There were plenty of objections to the plan, first and greatest that of cost, but there his good friends Chapman and Hall came to his assistance. They advanced him money on a new story to follow *Nicholas Nickleby*—say in November of the following year—and agreed to release him from further responsibility for *Master Humphrey's Clock*, which they brought to an end.

Catherine was horrified when she found that he

162

wanted her to go, too. She clung wildly to the hope that the expense would save her; and what would happen to their home and the children with both parents away? But Mrs. Macready offered to have the children, and Charles found a good tenant for the house. The mere thought of the voyage set Catherine crying, and she cried through all the final stages of preparation. To console her a little, their friend Maclise painted a picture of the children, with a new pet raven perched behind them. He had it fixed in a traveling case so that it could be set up conveniently wherever they happened to be, and in fact, they made it a little shrine before which they drank the children's health, accompanied occasionally by Charles playing *Home, Sweet Home* on an accordion.

They crossed the Atlantic in one of the new paddle steamers and had a frightful crossing. The paddleboxes were torn off and the lifeboats broken to bits. The crew said they had never known such a storm, and the captain assured the passengers that no sailing ship could have weathered it. Charles was sick six of the twenty days of the voyage. He then reappeared in the saloon, and passed some of the time playing whist; but "five or six times in the course of every rubber we were all flung from our seats, rolled out at different doors, and kept on rolling until we were picked up by stewards." They reached Boston most thankfully, and Charles was welcomed with wild enthusiasm as "the Nation's guest."

William Giles' old nickname, "the Inimitable," began to drop out of Charles' letters home with amusing effect. He wrote to Forster:

"I wish you could have seen the Inimitable shown to a great elbow chair by the Speaker's throne, and

sitting alone in the middle of the floor of the House
of Commons, the observed of all observers, and breaking in spite of himself into a smile as he thought of
this commencement to the Thousand and One Stories
in reserve for home and Lincoln's Inn Fields, and Jack
Straw's Castle—Ah, Forster, when I do come back
again!"

That exuberance did not last. The demands made
on him were so heavy. He could not escape the crowds
who recognized him everywhere from a portrait by
Maclise which had been widely published. They
mobbed him as the great Boz, creator of Little Nell,
Pickwick, Oliver and Nicholas. He marked the fact
that his books were as well known here as at home,
with the great difference that here they brought him
no financial return. The cheering and the flattery palled
on him. Half the purpose of his visit was being frus-
trated by this hero worship. How was he to get to
know the life of the people if he could never go among
them unrecognized?

All went well enough, however, until he touched
on the question of copyright agreement between the
two countries in a speech at a banquet given in his
honor. It gave offense and he was thought most un-
civil to speak of business affairs on such an occasion.
But, though he lost some sympathy, the lionizing went
on. Crowds continued to press as densely about him
wherever he went, and he traveled north to Canada
as well as out to the West. It was altogether more than
his nerves could stand. He grew irritable from fatigue,
lack of sleep and the loss of his privacy; and he became despondent as he felt the purpose of his visit
threatened with defeat. He wanted to write that book

about the Americans to pay for the visit, but how could he if he never met people on equal terms?

He and Catherine returned home after a stay of nearly six months in a sailing packet-ship—"none of your steamers this time," said Charles warily. They were both "fevered with anxiety to be home," and he planned to take his friends by surprise, arriving unannounced. The first Forster heard of it was the sound of Charles' familiar voice at Lincoln's Inn, as he ran upstairs one morning to greet him.

They had reached London in the middle of the night, but neither could rest till the children had been fetched home from Macready's house. The excitement of being dragged from his bed to see his parents sent little Charley into convulsions, but the other children were kissed and cried over without mishap.

Catherine's fourteen-year-old sister, Georgina, had been keeping an eye on them and had dropped in at the Macready's nearly every day. She had grown to be a great favorite with them all. She was now about the same age as Mary when Charles had first known her, and had the same sweet nature. She was so devoted to her nephews and nieces that she was soon spending weeks on end in her sister's household.

During his absence Charles had invented a whole new set of nicknames for the children. Charley had become "Flaster Floby," Katey the "Lucifer box" because of her hot temper, while sweet-tempered Mamey picked up for life the label of "Mild Gloster."

It was pleasant to be back among the old friends again, able to speak his mind without constraint and with no fear of being misunderstood. He had much to tell as they gathered at Forster's or Devonshire Place or elsewhere. Charles found he could not "dash at" the book about America. He had to consider how it would look to Americans as well as to readers at home. He wanted to write the truth as it seemed to him, and he needed advice. He discussed his material with Captain Marryat, the author of *Masterman Ready* and *The Children of the New Forest,* who knew the New World well; and his friends sat in committee with him on doubtful matters. He meant to dedicate it to "those friends of mine in America who, loving their country, can bear the truth when it is written goodhumoredly and in a kind spirit," but was dissuaded. *American Notes,* as he called it, has still a certain historical interest but has never been popular —nor was it the book Chapman and Hall were waiting for, as Charles was well aware.

It was actually not until November that he was able to put his mind to work on another story. He wrote then of having given himself up "to the agonies of plotting and contriving, in which state I am accustomed to walk up and down the house, smiting my forehead abjectly, and am so horribly cross and surly that the boldest fly at my approach." From such a description his near friends might have guessed that the story was not going well. He had set his hand to the plow, however, and *Martin Chuzzlewit* began to take shape.

The first number appeared in January, but to Charles' dismay sold little more than a quarter of the copies that had been sold each month of *Nicholas Nickleby.* He wondered if the public had come to prefer the shorter, weekly installments he had been publishing in *Master Humphrey's Clock,* and would no longer wait a month for the next part. Whatever the cause, the drop was too painfully apparent. *Chuz-*

zlewit was not earning anything like the money expected of it. The publishers naturally were disturbed, and Charles was baffled.

At first he blamed himself and tried to improve matters by introducing some of his experiences in America, but that brought no increase in the sales. The public did not even recognize Mrs. Gamp as one of his immortal characters, though this she soon became, with her invisible, but much quoted friend, Mrs. Harris, and such sayings as "Leave the bottle on the chimleypiece and let me put my lips to it when I feel so dispoged." Mrs. Gamp—fat, raucous, rednosed, moist-eyed, husky voiced, smelling of spirits, her dress stained with snuff, carrying a bundle, a pair of patterns and an old patched gig-umbrella—was not unusual as a nurse of the days before Florence Nightingale. For his picture of her, Charles made use of Miss Burdett Coutts' stories of a woman who had nursed her ex-governess.

When the agreement between Charles and his publishers had first been drawn up for *Martin Chuzzlewit,* a clause had been inserted to the effect that he would share the profits after a certain point with the publishers—or alternatively share any loss which might accrue. At the time, loss on any book by Boz sounded too unlikely to be considered. Now, with the story selling so poorly, both parties began to look a little blue. The idea that his inspiration might fail was sheer nightmare to Charles, as to anyone who tries to live by writing. Success had dropped out of the sky and he had taken it for granted. He was committed to a certain way of living, an expensive way. If his pen failed him, what would he do to keep his wife and four children—not to mention his parents?

Mrs. Gamp and friend, typical nurses before the days of
Florence Nightingale

During a conference between him and the publishers, Mr. Hall remarked that he hoped they might not have to ask Mr. Dickens to refund any of the money they had advanced on *Chuzzlewit* for him to go to America. Perhaps Charles should have laughed it off, but he was deeply worried. He was still, according to Forster, suffering "*Chuzzlewit* agonies." He was deeply shaken and very angry as he went out of the building, straight to Forster to tell him what had occurred, determined to repay every penny, but also to change his publishers.

Forster paced about the room in almost equal perturbation. He thought Charles foolish, but blamed the publishers as "bitter bad judges of an author." He knew, and they should, the sensitive intricacies of a writer's pride and vanity. Besides, as adviser to the firm, he owed a duty to both sides and was most unwilling to see them lose so valuable an author. He begged Charles to take no steps in the matter until after his autumn holiday, for time, he thought, puts most things in a better light. But, as so often before, Charles could not rest in a state of anxiety. He had been most appreciative of the unfailing kindness of Messrs. Chapman and Hall and, on the eve of his departure to America, had expressed his feelings in a grateful letter. He was as worried as anyone at the book's slow sales, but their appearance of having lost confidence in him wounded and humiliated him. In the future, he thought, he would try a different kind of arrangement. He asked Forster to make inquiries as to whether a firm of printers would publish for him. It was an awkward proposal, for they were largely employed by Chapman and Hall and, in their turn, would not want to risk offending a good customer. There were other difficulties as well, some quite serious ones, but Charles Dickens was important enough to get his own way. In the end his curious proposal was accepted.

He next turned to his private affairs and, in a state of great irritability, considered how best to economize. His horror of debt made him decide impetuously that he must go away where he could live cheaply. He could not go on living in his present beautiful home. It would have to be let. He made inquiries, and decided that Italy would probably suit him; but he was not quite ready to leave England yet. There were preparations to be made and he had engagements to fulfill. He had promised to make a tour of inspection of prisons to get information for Angela Burdett Coutts, and he was to speak at Birmingham and Manchester.

Manchester rewarded him with an idea. He had Disraeli and Cobden on his platform when he spoke on the value of education, and of ignorance as the fount of all evil. As he was driven through the city's busy streets, he watched the streams of people on the footpaths, rich and poor cut off from all neighborly feeling by ignorance of each other's lives, and by barriers of pride or poverty. If he could carry a story with a message of goodwill across the threshold of mansion and hovel alike, if it could be read by all around the fire at Christmas, might not those thorny barriers be broken down? Could he touch the stony hearts? He might at least warm the sad ones. So he conceived the idea of *A Christmas Carol*.

When he returned to London the story so took hold of him that he wrote it in a month, a month haunted by the figure of Scrooge, that "squeezing,

wrenching, grasping, scraping, clutching, covetous old
sinner, hard and sharp as flint; secret and self-con-
tained, and solitary as an oyster." In the small hours
of the night when his pen had run dry, he haunted
the city streets, seeing the scenes he was creating, the
ghosts of Scrooge and Marley, the old warehouse, and
the knocker on the front door, the little houses of
Camden Town and the limping figure of Tiny Tim.
He lost himself completely in the creation, writing
without a break until his mind went blank. He lived
the story through with Scrooge and suffered in each
of the tests to which the miser was submitted. He
kept away from his friends all that month. When it
was finished, he emerged triumphant, confident of
what he had done, ready to cast care aside and to
give himself up to a Christmas of all Christmasses.

Macready had gone to America that autumn and
Charles now set out to entertain the family he had left
behind. He arranged a giant party for Mrs. Macready
and the children. Half the famous people in London
were invited. He persuaded Forster to be his partner
in a grand exhibition of magic, learned for the occasion but highly successful. He had put all his worries
behind him and wrote hilariously to Mac of "such
dinings-out, such conjurings, such blind-man's buff-
ings, such theater-goings and such kissings-out of Old
Years, such kissings-in of New ones, as never took
place before."

Mrs. Carlyle was at the party, watching the fun
with a sardonic eye. She found herself caught up and
danced madly around by Charles so that, as she said
afterwards, she was afraid of having her brains knocked
out against the folding doors.

Charles never danced well but he enjoyed the frolic

of a bouncing polka or a swinging waltz. He had had all the children taught young, and one year Mamey and Katey tried to teach him to polka properly. However, although he submitted gravely to their instruction and practiced by himself in a corner as they ordered, he was never a credit to them.

Of all the festivals of the year, Christmas was dearest to Charles. It made him happy with an absurd, sentimental, bursting happiness which radiated out of him in good will towards all men, to the crossing sweeper every bit as much as to the comfortable friends of his drawing room. It was for him a time of open doors and greetings all along the street. For the children it meant the familiar round, shopping with father to choose presents for themselves and their friends, prickly holly with red berries, going to church and singing carols, Christmas dinner and the pudding brought in aflame with brandy, and all rising to the toast, "Here's to us all! God bless us!" And during the holiday season, parties, with charades or perhaps a play.

A *Christmas Carol* was the first of a series of Christmas stories. Each had its special purpose, but none of the others so nearly reflected Charles' own feelings. It was published by Chapman and Hall in spite of what had happened, but under a new agreement in which the usual conditions were reversed. Instead of the publishers paying the cost of making the book and the author drawing a royalty on every copy sold, Charles was to pay for the production and the publishers to draw the royalty. Charles apparently had not realized how heavy those initial costs would be, and he expected a nice fat check when the accounts were made up at the end of the year.

Unfortunately the little book came out late—only just in time for Christmas. There was no time to reprint it when the first edition sold out, so the check, when it came, was for only two hundred and thirty pounds ($1,150). He did not understand it, and felt very annoyed. However, he soon had something else to worry about. Almost as soon as the book was out it was pirated and appeared for sale in *Parley's Twopenny Illuminated Library* under the title of *A Christmas Ghost Story, re-originated from the Original by Charles Dickens and analytically condensed expressly for this work.*

Charles took immediate action. With Talfourd as his counsel, he obtained an injunction against the pirates, obliging them to stop publication. They fought the case, defending themselves on the grounds that they had also "re-originated" both *The Old Curiosity Shop* and *Barnaby Rudge* without the author's taking any action against them; and that in the case of *A Christmas Carol* they had "unhinged" it and put it together again with "its incongruities tastefully remedied!"

"They use my ideas as gipsies do stolen children," Charles protested in his plea against them, "they disfigure them and then make them pass for their own."

He claimed damages of a thousand pounds ($5,000) for they had sold their edition remarkably well; but the pirates took refuge in bankruptcy and Charles got nothing. He had even to pay the whole of his costs, which ran to over seven hundred pounds ($3,500).

"I shall not easily forget the expense, anxiety and horrible injustice of the *Carol* case," he wrote some time afterwards when he was refusing to take action for some later infringement of his copyrights.

Bewildered, aggrieved and really worried, he now set about the final arrangements for removing his great household to Italy. For one who had always worked so hard and was wholly dependent on writing, he had suffered some bad shocks during the past year, and he almost wondered whether bankruptcy lay ahead.

As he cast about for any way of making a little extra money, it occurred to him to propose some sketches of life abroad to one of the papers. He went to talk about it to the editor of *The Morning Chronicle*, no longer his old friend, Mr. Black, but a new man who told him ungraciously that he was asking too much, and declined the offer. Charles was not used to such treatment and vowed that he would never set foot in that office again. It looked as though nothing would go right for him these days, as though some spell had broken when he went to America, carrying all his luck with it.

~~~~~~

CHAPTER XVIII

"We Have Heard the Chimes at Midnight"

THE FAMILY WERE TO TRAVEL BY ROAD FROM CALAIS.
Preparations for the journey included a search for what
Charles described as "some good old shabby devil of
a coach" to carry the immense party to Genoa—Charles
and Catherine, five children, Georgina, Frederick,
nurses, servants, courier. He picked up a bargain, "about
the size of your library," he told Forster, fitted with
many pockets and "leathern cellars," lamps and an
arrangement on the roof for luggage.

At the port he stopped to change some English
money. As was then customary, he received it all in
five-franc (twenty-five-cent) pieces, two sackloads of
them! They set off behind four horses with nearly a
hundred bells jingling on their collars and in mid-
July reached safely the villa they had rented. It stood
among vineyards, facing the sea, "lonely, rusty, stag-
nant," wrote Charles, and so full of "vermin and
swarmers" that he half expected to see the carriage
carried off bodily by fleas. Yet they settled down and,
after he had tackled the language, he arranged pens
and paper before the window of the best bedroom
looking over the sea, and waited for inspiration—but
in vain.

The soil of Italy was alien to him. He missed his
London streets and found no compensation in the

Reading The Chimes *to friends at Forster's*

southern scene. The everlasting ringing of church bells maddened him and he thought yearningly of the English countryside and the "bright, lark-singing, coast-of-France-discerning days" at Broadstairs. Yet it was the bells of Genoa which gave him the idea for his new story. Exultant as the tide of words rose in him, he seized a sheet of paper and scribbled in the middle of it one line from *Henry IV* which he knew would wake echoes in Forster's breast.

"*We have heard the chimes at midnight, Master Shallow!*"

Yes, *The Chimes* was begun, and thereafter not all the bells in Europe could disturb him. What he heard was only the echo of those from the old London belfry of his imagination where Trotty Veck waited for his daughter. Again Charles meant to champion the poor and defenseless and to challenge the proud. He wrote confidently and tried each chapter on his family but, though their praise was pleasant, it did not satisfy him. As soon as the story was finished and sent off to the publishers, he yielded to the longing to hear his friends' opinion of it. He would take a holiday, visit Venice and Verona, and give himself one week—"to the hour"—in London. "And if you was a real gent," he wrote to Forster, "you'd get up a little circle for me one wet evening when I come!"

He met with frost and floods, and crossed over the Simplon Pass in the Alps by sleigh in fearful cold. Yet—"You know my punctiwality," he wrote again. "My design is to walk into Cuttris's coffee-room on Sunday the 1st of December, in good time for dinner, and shall look for you at the farther table by the fire."

True to his word, and buoyant as ever, he arrived. Forster arranged the "little circle" to hear the first reading of *The Chimes*. Maclise, as he listened, idly sketched the scene with his slightly mocking pencil, setting a sunburst over Charles' head and drawing Forster as a fat farmer, but leaving his personal impression of the moment to posterity.

The new book was in good time for Christmas and brought Charles a first check for fifteen hundred pounds ($7,500). Satisfied, he returned to the Continent. He stopped in Paris to see Macready, who was giving a short season of Shakespeare there. He was introduced to Dumas, Victor Hugo and Lamartine. Charles got on famously with them. In mid-December he was back with his family in Genoa.

Six months later he decided that his economies had gone far enough and the immense party set out again thankfully for home. Charles at once embarked on a brilliant season of amateur theatricals for charity. The play they chose was Ben Jonson's *Every Man in His Humour*. He and Forster took principal parts; acting with them were four famous artists, Cruikshank, Maclise, John Leech and Frank Stone. Macready was persuaded to coach them, and forgot his first reluctance as he saw how hard Charles made them work and how well he himself shaped up. The performance was an out-and-out success, and requests for it to be repeated came from all over the country. It was given at Liverpool, Manchester, Birmingham, and everywhere was received with great enthusiasm.

This was the first of a number of theatrical engagements on which Charles and his friends embarked during the next twenty years with almost professional zeal. New friends joined the original company, notably Wilkie Collins and John Tenniel.

Charles had hardly been three weeks at home before he was planning a new story, *The Cricket on the Hearth*, the third of the Christmas books. It had some bad reviews but sold like hot cakes, and was being acted in twelve London theaters before the year was out.

Greatly contented, and refreshed by the quiet time abroad, he was soon feeling the stir of new ideas. Something more startling than anything he had imagined before emerged. He conceived the idea of a new daily paper and worked on plans in secret with Douglas Jerrold and W. H. Wills, both famous journalists. He sought information about newspaper organization, and became dazzled by the scale of the enterprise. Backers were found and Charles himself, as "the champion of progress and reform," was invited to be the paper's first editor. He accepted the position and contributed a great deal to the initial policy of the paper, which was the *Daily News*. He was offered a salary of two thousand pounds ($10,000) a year, and rejoiced to think of such security for himself, thinking that he would still have time to go on writing. He brought his father back from Devonshire to be in charge of the reporters' room. He made Kate's father dramatic critic. He hoped to find a place for Tom Beard.

Before the first issue appeared, however, financial troubles in the City damped the backers' enthusiasm. Charles got a disquieting glimpse of the other side of the proposition, and did not like the feeling of a master at his heels. He saw that he would not be able to go his own way unchecked, even as editor. Also, his curiosity had now been satisfied and his interest in the great project was fading. He resigned three weeks after the first number was published.

He was widely blamed for his irresponsibility; but much as he would have liked it, the position was too heavy and the task too impersonal to be handled successfully by one of his temperament. The very qualities which had made him famous would have been wasted there. Forster had had doubts of his wisdom in attempting it from the beginning, and it was he who took his place as editor.

After his resignation Charles contributed three important letters to the paper on the question of capital punishment, on which he held strong views. He was sufficiently ahead of his time to advocate its total abolition, but he was practical enough to see that the public generally was not ready for that and he must go one step at a time. He opened fire therefore against *public* executions. He had been present at many both in London and abroad, and had observed the mood of the crowds who stood in line all night long for a good place and passed the time drinking and roistering. They greeted the prisoner on his way to the scaffold with shrieks and catcalls and, amid ribald laughter, watched him die. In order to understand as well as he could the feelings of the condemned, Charles had talked also to wardens, chaplains, even to the hangman himself.

Three years later other letters from him on the same subject appeared in *The Times;* but it was another twenty years before the law was changed, even to the provision that the death sentence should be carried out behind prison walls.

The comfortable editor's salary came to an end, of course, with his resignation from the paper, and he had to look closely at his money affairs. Again it seemed prudent to go abroad. This time he chose

Switzerland, to which the family traveled by steamer down the Rhine. The news of his presence soon brought crowds along the shore to hail the genius who had given them "the immortal Pickwick." His books were already well known in Germany and over much of the Continent, including Russia. The Germans found him extraordinarily young, and so domestic, with his enormous family.

A new story had been pricking at his imagination before he left London, "a study in pride." As always when inspiration burned, he fretted to get to work on it. First, however, he had to report to Lord John Russell about the Ragged Schools into which he had been inquiring for Angela Burdett Coutts. He had also set himself to write the story of the New Testament for his children, and had to finish that before he could count himself free. Then he began *Dombey.*

It came easily at first and he was pleased with it. The first part came out in October and was "a prodigious success." Much that had been stored away in Charles' memory since childhood went into it. He recalled the walks to Limehouse to visit his godfather, and the little wooden midshipman in Leadenhall Street which he had come to love like an old friend, so that whenever he passed, he used to stop to pat it. Sol Gills and Captain Cuttle also came out of the same period, as did Mrs. Pipchin, keeper of that "infantine boarding house" to which Paul Dombey was sent—though in such different circumstances from those in which Charles had known the original of that character.

He was no sooner deep in *Dombey* than it broke on him that if there was to be a Christmas book that

The little wooden midshipman in Threadneedle Street, close to where the Beadnells lived

year, he must begin it at once. He was extroardinarily
unwilling to break off the tale which was going so
well. He doubted whether he could run the two together as he used to do in his early writing days. His
mind was so full of *Dombey,* he could find only
shadowy, wispy ideas for the other. He tried now this,
now that, but his heart was not in them. He had suggested a sort of battleground idea to Forster months
earlier, and he hammered away to get something out
of it now. It came into being as *The Battle of Life,*
which proved quite successful and made a good deal
of money, but neither he nor his friends ever cared
much for it. As soon as it was out of the way, he
returned thankfully to the novel.

He was living outside Lausanne, and made many
friends there, among them the director of a school for
the blind in which he became immensely interested.
But the new friends did not make up for the old,
and he longed for those friendly critics whose judgment was so valuable to him. Nevertheless he began
to read his work aloud to the new circle and found
their shrewdness stimulating, so that he took new pleasure in making the scenes live for them. It seemed to
give him a different feeling about his characters, as
though each were speaking in his own right through
Charles' mouth. He found himself almost acting the
scenes, and felt the drama of the situations strengthened thereby.

He saw his audience hanging on his words, entirely
under his spell, and found he could move them at will
to tears or laughter. It was a strange power and curiously exhilarating. He began to wonder whether larger
audiences would yield to it, and how such an idea
might be received in London. He sounded out Forster,

writing to him, "In these days of lecturings and readings, a great deal of money might possibly be made by one's having Readings of one's own books. It would be an *odd* thing. I think it would take immensely. What do you say?"

Forster thought it would be entirely beneath the dignity of a gentleman!

CHAPTER XIX

~~~~~~

David Copperfield

WHEN THE WEATHER SHOWED SIGNS OF BREAKING, Charles felt quite ready to leave Lausanne. *Dombey* was so far written that he was not afraid of the interruption, so "with several tons of luggage, other tons of servants and other tons of children," his extraordinary cavalcade set out and reached Paris in five days. "We got through the journey charmingly," he wrote, "though not quite as quickly as we hoped. The children as good as usual and Skittles (the new baby) jolly to the last. I call him so from something skittle-playing and public-housey in his countenance. We have been up at five every morning and on the road before seven. We were three carriages—a sort of wagon with a cabriolet attached for the luggage, a ramshackle old swing upon wheels (hired at Geneva) for the children, and for ourselves, the traveling chariot."

They broke the journey in Paris, staying first in a hotel, then taking a furnished house. They remained there for three months, very sociably, going often to the theater and entertaining other writers and actors. Here Charles received sad news that Fanny, his sister, had collapsed while singing at Manchester. Some time earlier he had feared she was going into a decline, and had persuaded her to see a specialist who had at that time been able to reassure them. Now he arranged for her to see him again, and found that she was far gone in consumption.

She died in the following July. Charles spent a good deal of time with her during the last weeks of her illness. He was a good sickroom visitor, and there was much sympathy and understanding between him and his sister. She was thirty-nine, and had been happy both in her musical career and her marriage. She had several children, the last only a few months old. She found it hard to reconcile herself to the idea of leaving them all and went through a period of bitter rebellion. But she schooled herself and was, in the end, able to say that she felt no more sadness in dying, except that, in the natural order of events, it must be such a very long time before she saw any of them again.

She and Charles talked much about themselves. He had already been exploring his memories to write *Dombey,* and must have recalled many that only Fanny shared—though perhaps more than even she had never known. Together they must have remembered those Sundays they had spent at the Marshalsea, and of how particular he had been to appear spick and span when he went to fetch her from the Academy of Music— but how little she still knew of how he had spent the other days of those weeks.

What had inspired that deep reserve which had lasted right up to the present? Wounded vanity? Some feeling of betrayal which kept him from trusting anyone with the truth? Why had the hurt gone so deep? Partly I think because of his imagination, always so lurid and so strong. He could still frighten himself with it after he was grown up. When his mother fled to join her husband in the Marshalsea, he had felt abandoned, pushed out of the nest before he was ready to fly. He remembered what he had seen with James in Seven Dials and his imagination turned it into pictures of "indescribable wickedness." His grief at having his education cut short had been bitter, for his dreams had been destroyed thereby, and by the parents he loved and trusted. He was certainly no coward, and he did not wilt in adversity. He remained kind and eager, still interested in the world about him in spite of misery which might have made him self-centered. Probably his inability to confide in his parents convinced him that no one else would understand cither. He hid his misery from the world, but hugged it to himself and became too conscious of it, and those feelings tended later to color his treatment of any young characters in his stories in whom he saw his own experiences reflected; for example Oliver, David, Pip. He exaggerated their defenselessness and gentility, and shielded them too pitifully from the world he chose to make hard for them. But what a contrast between those far-off days and the present, with the "Inimitable," famous, respected, secure, with a well-cared-for family, fine house, carriages and horses.

Stirred by his talks with Fanny, he now wrote to Forster—"Shall I leave you my life in manuscript when I die?" but he gave no clue then of what he had to tell. It happened at this time that another figure popped up out of that jealously hidden past. One day Forster received a quizzical inquiry as to whether the famous Boz could be the son of John Dickens, once of the Navy Pay Office, the same poor lad who had once been seen working in a factory window in Chandos Street.

Taken by surprise, Charles denied it, but returned

with the bare truth. After that, the thought of using his early experiences possessed him, and so *David Copperfield* began to take shape, not as an autobiography but as something "ingeniously done, with a very complicated inter-weaving of truth and fiction."

A story written for serialization had to have a title almost as soon as it was conceived and, in Charles' case, before the plot had taken shape so he had his usual difficulty in finding one to his taste. At first he called the hero David Mag, and suggested *Mag's Diversions* as the title, though he was afraid it might sound rather "too comic." He was reluctant to discard it altogether, as it offered him many opportunities for quips and jokes for a *mag* was slang for a halfpenny as well as short for a magpie. Then Mag became Copperfield (perhaps because a halfpenny is a copper), and everyone was satisfied. It was not until Forster pointed it out that Charles realized that the hero now had his own initials in reverse.

He made young David's circumstances more romantic than his own, and thrust him out into the world more dramatically and at an earlier age. Hablot Browne's drawing of him in Miss Trotwood's parlor, wrapped in shawls, makes him ridiculously young for the run of the text up to that point, yet Charles must have passed it for he examined all the illustrations for his books very critically. It is especially interesting in that connection to find that his comment on the first sketch of Mr. Micawber was "Capital! Uncommonly characteristic!"—which suggests that it was characteristic of John Dickens also.

It is not very surprising that, though he knew well enough what he wanted to do, Charles had found it difficult to get this very personal story started and

complained about "lumbering on like a stage wagon."
However, by November it was going well and he
could say, "I am wonderfully in harness. Nothing galls
or frets." He had been to Suffolk for the setting at
Blundestone of The Rookery, and to Yarmouth for the
Peggotty's home in an up-turned boat.

He meant his portrait of little Em'ly to carry a deep
moral, and expressed a hope that he might perhaps
be remembered for that, if for nothing more, in years
to come. He wanted to make people look at the reality
behind the common conventions, and to see behind
the story of the "fallen woman" the inner life of that
child of the Yarmouth shore.

Bitter-sweet memories of Maria went to the making of Dora with, surely, some glimpses of his own
early married life in the "beautiful, comic love" between her and David. He could not forget Maria's
jilting him, and he could not make up his mind what
to do with her. The words, "I have still Dora to kill"
drop oddly out of one of his letters.

One of the sturdiest of Dickens' female characters
was Betsy Trotwood. She was drawn from a woman
who lived in a little house facing the sea at Broadstairs,
almost next door to the Albion Hotel where Charles
stayed so often and wrote some chapters of *Copperfield*. Stories of her cantankerousness over the question of donkeys on the green lingered long after her
death, and Charley Dickens remembered being chased
off by her very indignantly with a hearth brush when
a donkey ran away with him across the strip of grass
she guarded so jealously. The house still stands almost
untouched. You can look over the gate, as the fam-
ished David did, to the parlor window and above it
to the one from which Mr. Dick goggled at the boy

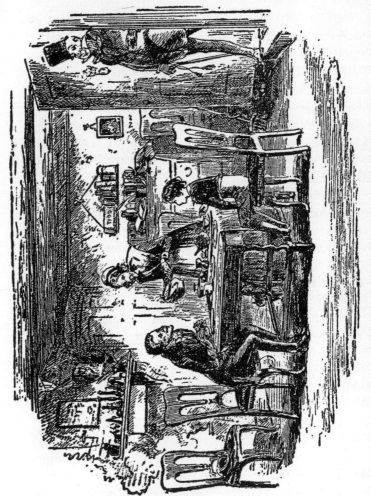

Enter Mr. Micawber—"an uncommonly characteristic" likeness

below. Behind the bay window to the right of the front door is the little room with the tall press built into the wall, from which Miss Trotwood brought her odd selection of restoratives when David fainted. Up under the roof is the little attic where David was put to bed and lay looking through the low window at the moonlight across the sea.

Charles was so accustomed to writing from his own observations of real life that he sometimes overstepped the mark, and found himself charged with libel. It happened with Miss Mowcher in this book and in *Bleak House,* with Harold Skimpole, thought to be Leigh Hunt, a well-known writer. As he had used his own parents in *Copperfield,* he was surprised and impatient when objections were raised. As soon as he realized, however, that his portrait of Miss Mowcher had given pain to its original, he was full of contrition, and did his best to undo the mischief. So it was that, after his first unforgettable description of the lively little dwarf, bubbling over with mischief, standing on a table to tend Steerforth's handsome locks and punctuating her scandalous conversation with "Ain't I volatile, Mr. Copperfield?"—Miss Mowcher was carefully transformed into a benevolent nonentity, of no interest to anyone.

At length, the end in sight, Charles wrote to Forster, "I am within three pages of the shore, and am strangely divided as usual between sorrow and joy. Oh, my dear Forster, if I were to say half of what *Copperfield* makes me feel tonight, how strangely, even to you, I should be turned inside out! I seem to be sending some part of myself into the shadowy world."

The publication of *Copperfield* brought Maria Beadnell back from the past. Charles had been out of town and, glancing through the pile of letters which had accumulated during his absence, he came on one in her handwriting. He felt a boy again as he picked it up. In imagination he saw a dramatic meeting between them. She was now married, and Charles immediately sent Catherine to call so that an invitation to dinner could be sent. But when he looked upon his old love, on the arm of her husband, no vision from the past came to sustain him. It was very much as he described Arthur Clennam's meeting with Flora Finching in *Little Dorrit*—"His passion shivered and broke to pieces. Flora, always tall, had grown to be very broad, too, and short of breath—but that was not much. Flora whom he had left a lily, had become a peony—that was not much. Flora who had seemed enchanting in all she said and thought, was diffuse and silly. That was much. Flora who had been spoiled and artless long ago, was determined to be spoiled and artless now. That was a fatal blow."

In February John Dickens died. He had been suffering for some time from an internal complaint of which he had said nothing to his family. An operation was attempted, but was unsuccessful. This was still before the days of anesthetics and Charles, observing the fortitude with which his father bore his pain, felt all his old affection and admiration welling up in him. He forgot the bad times and remembered only a lifetime of good humor and kindness. The old, absurd flourishes of speech which were put so effectively into Micawber's mouth in *Copperfield* rang through Charles' head with a new and gallant sound. He recalled the zeal with which his father had thrown himself into other people's affairs (though never, alas, into his own) and, as a last tribute to him, he chose the phrase, "a zealous, useful, cheerful spirit."

It was about this time that Sir Edward Bulwer (afterwards Lord) Lytton, with Charles, Forster and other distinguished men, was working to provide a kind of Provident Society for members of the artistic professions who so often fell on bad times, without resources to tide themselves over until fortune smiled again. Charles was always very much aware of the hazards and chances of the artist's life and gave the project his full support. He liked to cite Samuel Johnson as a case in point, asking did not he sell his rights in *Rasselas* to pay for his mother's funeral? (And, indeed, that is what Dr. Johnson, the most sought-after literary figure of his time in England, had had to do.)

It was to be called the Guild of Literature and Art. To help raise funds for it, Lytton presented some of his land which was to provide a site for houses for poor members of these professions. Actors promised to put on special performances for it and Charles happily set about reviving *Every Man in His Humor*, with himself and his friends in their old parts. It was produced at Knebworth (Lytton's great house). In the following year the same distinguished band of amateurs performed a play by Lytton himself, called *Not So Bad As We Seem*. During the month of the opening of the Great Exhibition in Hyde Park, they presented the play before Queen Victoria and the Prince Consort at Devonshire House.

Charles frankly delighted in having so good a pretext for the amateur theatricals he so much enjoyed. The play was taken on tour to many towns throughout the country—a triumphant tour it was and Forster refers to it as Dickens' "splendid strolling."

The funds for the Guild thus grew steadily, but the writers, painters and actors for whom it had been designed hung back. They never really accepted the idea, preferring to starve in their own way. But out of it grew the Royal Literary Fund to which many emi‑nent writers have had cause to be grateful.

CHAPTER XX

Public Readings

IN 1850, CHARLES STARTED ANOTHER MAGAZINE, HOUSE-*hold Words,* which like *Master Humphrey's Clock* was to be cheap and both entertaining and instructive so as to appeal to the whole family. It was a great success, and he was a good editor, quick to recognize talent and generous to young writers. Of the novel, *Cranford,* which Mrs. Gaskell, its author, sent him for a serial, he could only murmur, "Perfect, perfect!"

The lease of his house in Devonshire Terrace was coming to an end, but he already had his eye on Tavistock House in Bloomsbury. It was neither as large nor as handsome as the other, but had one advantage —a room on the first floor which could be made into a private theater. Many plays were performed in it, and with such success that "Dickens' first nights" were treated by the press almost as seriously as professional ones. Twelfth Night parties generally included a play in which all the Dickens children took part—and they were Charley, Mamey, Katey, Walter, Francis, Alfred, Sydney, Henry, and, in 1852, Edward. The latter acquired and kept the nickname of Mr. Plornishmaroontigoonter, Plorn for short. He made "positively his first appearance on any stage" at the age of three.

Charles coached everyone in their parts, and they were properly made up. During one of their most successful shows Thackeray, among the audience, laughed so uproariously that he fell off his chair.

Towards the autumn of 1851 Charles was seized "with such a torment of desire to be anywhere but where I am, that it is like being driven away." A plot for a new story possessed him and he craved solitude in order to develop it, conjuring up visions of remote valleys in the Swiss mountains where strong winds blew and he could be alone—but that could not be, and it was in London that he began to write this great novel, *Bleak House*, with its unforgettable picture of one of the old "London particulars" descending on the City and spreading up river and down, over the Essex marshes and the Kentish heights, inflaming eyes and throats and nipping fingers and toes; and, in the pit of the fog, the Court of Chancery, somber and sinister, "with its decaying houses and blighted lands in every shire, its worn-out lunatic in every madhouse, its dead in every churchyard." Reports of a recent law suit had set him on fire and he was as eloquent as John the Baptist calling the world to repentance.

He had no difficulty this time in getting into the story. His pen raced over the page; but he found he tired more quickly and had lost much of his old resilience. It worried him and he suspected that he was overworking. Certainly the magazine made heavy demands on his time, and he wrote a good deal for it. He was also following the Scripture book for his children with an English History as he found none to his liking. Most important of all, probably, was the preparation of readings from his books which he was working on in spite of all his friends' objections. They sapped him emotionally, but he was determined to give them a trial. He did so at Birmingham in December, 1853, when he read A *Christmas Carol* and *The Cricket on the Hearth* to raise funds for a Working Men's Institute.

He had pruned the text carefully, omitting all that he could convey by voice or gesture, and he rehearsed as carefully as for a theatrical production. They were successful beyond any doubt. The audiences were spellbound from first to last. So many people had to be turned away at the doors that he gave an extra performance at reduced prices for working men and their wives only. The funds gained between four and five hundred pounds, Dickens taking nothing for himself.

During the next five years he went all over the country giving such readings in aid of good causes, and everywhere people flocked to hear him and showed an appreciation which touched him deeply. He then resolved to give a season of readings in London for his own benefit, and felt justified by the rush for tickets. Even the critical found themselves swept away by his performance.

Thomas Carlyle said, "I had no conception before hearing Dickens read, what capacities lie in the human face and voice." The great actor, Macready, went again and again, admiring the genius of the performances, moved by it to tears and then to laughter.

An American lady wrote that he brought the scenes so vividly to life that often she found it hard to believe that the words he used were really there in the book, till she looked them up afterwards. She felt this with his description of the Peggottys' boat-house, and of Lant Street where Bob Sawyer entertained the Pickwickians to supper. She described Charles reading about the Micawbers, tipping backwards and forwards on heels and toes as he twisted an eyeglass or gestured as with a punch ladle, his cheeks almost seeming to become apoplectic and to be fenced in by a wall of shirt collar as he spoke in the thin throaty tones of Mr. Micawber, breaking off into coughs which seemed inseparable from his speech and choked it into silence; and how he changed into Mrs. Micawber, sipping her punch, smoothing her hair, as she blandly discussed her husband's prospects.

When he gave *A Christmas Carol,* he lowered his brows and used a harsh, vibrating tone as he read, *"Ah, but he was a tight-fisted hand at the grindstone, was Scrooge."*

Charles always read with a script before him but rarely referred to it. He stood before a dark curtain, at a simple desk which held his books and a glass of water. His voice carried without any sort of amplifier and he held audiences of as many as 3,000 people for as long as two hours at a stretch. He set before them the familiar stories as he meant them to be understood, marking the humor and the pathos, miming sublimely each of the characters. *Dombey* was such a favorite that "we could stay here a week with that one reading," he wrote from Dublin, and "I have never seen men cry so undisguisedly" (as at little Paul's death). "As to *Mrs. Gamp*—it was just one roar with me and with them, for they made me laugh so that sometimes I could not compose my face to go on."

He told Forster (who had thought it an ungentlemanly thing to do) of the demonstrations of affection and respect wherever he went. "The deepest and most uncomfortably packed crowd will be hushed in an instant when I show my face. Common people and gentle folk stop me in the streets and say, 'Mr. Dickens, will you let me touch the hand that has filled my home with so many friends?'"

On his forty-second birthday Charles, now with a "satanic, flowing mustache," asked Tom Beard to come and tramp with him from Gravesend to Rochester and back by Cobham Woods. It was a fine sunny morning as they came down the Dover Road and there, opposite the house on Gadshill, was a board announcing land for sale. It brought him to a standstill and all his old feeling for the neighborhood rushed over him.

As soon as he got back to town he made inquiries about it, but found he was too late. The plot was gone, but the house itself was for sale. It was with a little quiver of superstitious feeling that he told his agent to negotiate for it, to haggle a little, for he would not seem too eager. In fact he paid only ten pounds less than was asked—and he signed the check for it on a Friday! He told himself coolly that he would put it in order and let it furnished most of the year—but he became too fond of it. He let it only once, for a few weeks, and it became his home as no other house had been. He grew into it, and even now, though it has been a girls' school for some years, it seems still to breathe memories of Dickens.

One morning when he was in the City on business connected with the lease, he went across the river to see what was left of the Marshalsea, lately pulled down. The great gates and the spike-topped walls were gone, but the room in which he had watched the signing of the petition remained intact. He went into it and felt himself a boy again with his father and all that shabby company. Memories swept over him so that, for a moment, he felt he must possess it, rent it, to keep them alive. But, as he went away, he knew it had already given him all it had to offer. Out of that moment grew the story of "the father of the Marshalsea"

Gadshill Place

and *Little Dorrit,* but he could not decide how to use the material. He made several false starts before he hit on the happy device of bringing a number of the characters together by chance on the Continent and letting the reader see how their futures were intertwined. In it is his memorable and satirical picture of the "Circumlocution Office."

Charles had allowed the old clergyman, who was living at Gadshill Place when he bought it, to move when he pleased. This was not until the summer of 1857. Plans for modernizing the house and for painting and decorating were ready and an army of workmen took possession immediately. A better water supply was required for his new bathrooms and kitchens, and boring began and was continued for many months. The old stables were pulled down and new ones built.

The coach house made way for a servants' hall with a good large room over it for the boys to play in, at a suitable distance from their father's study.

He could not wait for the work to be finished. He came and picnicked among the builders, rather enjoying the racket in spite of an occasional grumble. His immense pleasure was soon plain in letters to friends all over the world. He boasted modestly of "my little Kentish freehold, looking on as pretty a view as you will find in a long day's English ride, a grave, red brick house, pleasantly irregular." He delighted to tell the tale of Sir John Falstaff and Gadshill. "The robbery was committed before the door," one runs, "and Falstaff ran away from the identical spot of ground now covered by the room in which I write. A little rustic alehouse called the Sir John Falstaff is over the way in honor of the event. Cobham Woods are behind the house, the distant Thames in front, the Medway with Rochester on one side. The whole stupendous property is on the old Dover Road."

The railway pleased him, too. It had already reached Gravesend and was shortly to be extended to Higham, only a mile or so from his house. He was soon a familiar sight on the road in his basket phaeton drawn by the horse he called Newman Noggs, with two big dogs following and lifting their heads from time to time for a pat.

One of the first distinguished guests at "Gads" was Hans Christian Andersen. Ten years earlier he had sent Dickens a copy of the English translation of his fairy tales. Charles was enchanted with them, especially with *The Little Tin Soldier*. So when he was coming to England, Andersen asked a mutual friend to introduce them because "when I read his books I often think that I have seen such things, and feel I could write like that. Do not misunderstand me—I do not know how better to express myself. As the wind whistled round his bell rope (in *The Chimes*), I have often heard it whistle on a cold wet evening, and the chirp of the cricket I well remember in the cosy corner of my parents' humble home."

Andersen was an awkward fellow, very tall, all elbows, knees and long irregular features. He was unpredictable in his reactions and abnormally sensitive, so lost in his own imagination that he found it difficult to know what was expected of him. He was a trial to the Dickens boys, expecially to Charley whom he requested to shave him every morning; but he got on well with Catherine and used to pick little nosegays in the woods for her. He delighted the younger children with his delicate cut-out pictures of elves, gnomes, sprites, trees and flowers.

He would dearly have liked to wander with Boz through the London of his books, but his oddity made such an idea unpracticable. He would have been too conspicuous. He might also have taken fright at what he saw, for he was very nervous. Once when they were going to London together, Andersen got lost on London Bridge Station, found a cab for himself and drove off to their meeting place. The cabby took him by way of the half-made streets of Clerkenwell. Andersen fell into a panic, imagining he was being driven out to some lonely place to be robbed and probably murdered. He undid his boots and stuffed into them his money, watch and papers. When the cab stopped, Charles, waiting anxiously for him, saw him hobble out, hardly able to walk and speechless with fright.

CHAPTER XXI

Gadshill

BEFORE HE SETTLED IN THE NEW HOUSE, CHARLES FOUND he had a desperate personal problem to face. More than once in recent months he had confided in Forster his growing fear of a breakdown, though that was not the root of it. The fantastic pressure at which he had worked for so long was certainly telling on him, and he was never free from the fear that inspiration might fail and he would discover himself with nothing more to write. It had been partly as a second string to his bow that he had taken up the readings, but those had also taken their heavy toll of time and strength. He was often tempted to run away, to find some remote spot where he could think and see his life in a proper perspective—"Restlessness, you will say," he wrote to Forster. "Whatever it is, it is always driving me and I cannot help it." But it was more than that.

A little later, "in a dishevelled state of mind," he was asking "Why is it that, as with poor David (Copperfield), a sense comes always crushing on me now when I fall into low spirits, as of one happiness I have missed in life, one friend and companion I have never met?"

If only he could tear himself free, he thought he would like to go and live for a while with the Brothers in the Hospice at the St. Bernard's Pass. Then ruefully he told himself that it was probably "better to go on and fret than to stop and fret; and as for repose, for some men there's no such thing in the world."

It was in such a troubled state of mind that he brought himself at last to confide in Forster and told him that he believed he and Catherine must part.

"It is not only that she makes me uneasy and unhappy, but that I made her so too, and much more so," he wrote. "She is exactly what you know in the way of being amiable and complying, but we are strangely assorted for the bond there is between us. God knows she would have been a thousand times happier if she had married another kind of man. I am often cut to the heart by thinking what a pity it is, for her own sake, that I ever fell in her way. If I were sick or disabled tomorrow, I know how sorry she would be. But the incompatibility would arise the moment I was well again. I know you cannot help me. Why I have even written, I hardly know, but it is a miserable sort of comfort that you should be clearly aware how matters stand."

It was a sorry business and Catherine suffered in her way as much as Charles. Without knowing a great deal more of the circumstances, it is hard to see how the situation came about after their twenty years of marriage and with nine children to be considered. Divorce was unthinkable then, and it was evidently not simply that Charles wanted to be free to live his own life. For all his longing for silence and solitude, he kept the children with him and was as tied as ever.

Catherine went away unhappily, weeping and probably not understanding what it was all about. There is no doubt that she loved Charles, but so much of his life she had not even wanted to share. She had none of his vitality—how much difference even a little would have made! She seemed incapable of putting up a fight for herself, could neither reason nor explain; could only feel blindly and weep.

To Charles a state of indecision was always unbearable and, having made up his mind to a course of action, he could not rest until it was accomplished. When he had faced the position, what he wanted was a separation, final, and legally arranged, and he immediately set proceedings in motion, asking Forster to act for him and Mark Lemon for Catherine. There was great resentment among the Hogarths, especially as Georgina would not desert Charles and the children and was, consequently, estranged from her family for a while.

Charles made Catherine an allowance of six hundred pounds a year, and took a house for her near Regents Park, to which he sent Charley, with instructions to look kindly after his mother.

When some of the anguish had faded, Catherine gathered together his letters. She made them into a bundle, as a sort of talisman against despair, a proof, she said, that he had once loved her. Among them were those quoted earlier, written before their marriage, and showing how difficult their relationship had been even then. The children went freely to see her in her new home, and her daughters spoke lovingly of her in their Recollections—but of the full, happy life that was being established at Gadshill, Catherine knew almost nothing.

During the rest of that year, and much of the next, Charles was constantly traveling about the country, giving readings. He read in London every Thursday in July and at the beginning of August set out for a four months' tour of England, Ireland and Scotland, during the whole of which he gave four or five readings a week. It may possibly have served to distract him from the effects of the upheaval in his life, but can only have increased that exhausting restlessness of which he had complained, and the sense of strain. Indeed, Forster, in his forthright way, blamed the readings for much of his friend's unhappy state of mind. On such tours, he lived too much on his nerves. About this time Forster himself got married, and thereafter the friends saw less of one another.

It was a relief when, next spring, ideas for another book presented themselves and Charles was able to lose himself in working out a plot. *A Tale of Two Cities* had been gathering substance in his mind ever since he first read Carlyle's *French Revolution*. For sheer story-telling it has always held its readers. As a play it has been revived many times on stage, screen and on radio.

Times had now changed indeed! For the privilege of publishing this book serially one day after the installment appeared in England, an American firm paid him $5,000.

Once when he was in the north on a reading tour, with a long empty evening ahead of him, Charles sent the porter from his hotel out for something to read—anything by Sir Walter Scott, he said, or even something of his own. The man came back with a copy of *The Old Curiosity Shop* and over a roaring fire Charles read it with growing hilarity—not on account of the story itself, but because of the memories it evoked of the circumstances in which it had been written. As soon as he got back to London he set out to re-visit some of the old haunts and found that one thing led

to another quite entrancingly. It was a good cure for
his state of mind and he began to write down the new
impressions and his memories of old ones. Out of these,
too, grew a book which he called *The Uncommercial
Traveller*. For the curious and inquiring reader there
is a great deal of autobiographical material to be
gleaned from it, an account of the games he made
out of his early reading at Chatham for Fanny and
the Stroughills and many other pictures of life in that
town. There are glimpses of himself as a clerk in Gray's
Inn, of his courting of Maria—and of the "shabby old
devil of a coach" in which he and his family had
traveled to Italy in 1844.

It was while he was thus delving into the past that
he wrote to Angela Burdett Coutts about Gadshill and
described how as a very odd little boy, trudging thither
from Chatham beside his father, he must have had the
first faint shadows of all his books already in his head.

Household Words was still thriving. Several of his
own stories ran through it as serials; so did two of
Wilkie Collins' most famous novels, *The Moonstone*
and *The Woman in White*.

Collins had met Charles in the days of his "splendid
strolling" and they were now excellent friends. Charles
enjoyed Wilkie's feeling for melodrama. Some of his
friends said he was too much influenced by it. Forster
could not bear the man and made no secret of his
feelings, but Forster's marriage kept him more and
more from his old friends, and Charles came to discuss
work and ideas with Wilkie instead.

Charles had now given up Tavistock House, feeling
that he did not need a town house as well as a country
one. He kept two or three rooms in Wellington Street,

Strand, over the offices of *All the Year Round* where he could stay for a night or two when he wished. Occasionally he took furnished houses when he needed to entertain or wished to give Mamey some amusement and gaiety, but Gadshill was definitely and finally his home. He was happy there and enjoyed a contentment he had seldom found elsewhere.

In the course of the years he made many improvements to the house. He also bought a piece of land on the other side of the road, under which he had a tunnel dug so that he could reach the new plot without going outside his own property. There, among fine trees, he erected a Swiss chalet which a great friend and admirer, the German actor Fechter, had sent him —in ninety-four pieces, which fitted together as easily as a child's puzzle. It stood two stories high, and round the walls of the upper room, which became his summer work room, he fixed five large mirrors to catch the reflections of the swaying branches of the trees, of birds and butterflies, and even of distant cornfields and the waters of the Medway.

Gadshill Place, though now a girls' school, keeps something of the atmosphere Dickens gave it. The tunnel still leads under the road into the pleasant shrubbery. (The chalet has been removed to Cobham Park.) To the right of the front door as you enter the house is his study, with some sham bookshelves he had made for his study door in Tavistock House. They were one of his little jokes, and the titles he invented for the book backs still raise a smile. In the gardens are the graves of many household pets—dogs, cats, ravens, all loved in their time by Charles and his children, and buried there by them.

It was a common saying in those parts that no one

The John Falstaff Inn, Gadshill

ever passed the Sir John Falstaff so long as he had a
penny in his pocket! Hop pickers in their season
streamed down the Dover Road, and stopped there.
Tramps, gypsies, fair and circus folks encamped
round it. Charles kept good dogs to protect his home
and family, but he liked to wander among the rogues
and vagabonds in his old way, and to talk to them.

From Gadshill he covered many miles over which
his smaller feet had walked years before. He lingered
over Rochester's old stones and timbered houses, looked
again into the Dockyard and still saw romance in its
myriad activities. He walked over Cooling Marshes and
looked at the grave in the churchyard with the "little
stone lozenges about a foot long . . . arranged in a neat
row" (thirteen of them, not the mere five he mentioned
in the story he was meditating), as "sacred to the
memory of five little brothers, born on their backs

with their hands in their trouser pockets." Again the Dockyard reminded him of the "hulks" and the shackled men working there—and the story of Pip and the gravestones, Pip and the Gargerys, Pip and Magwich, grew into *Great Expectations.*

It was a story which pleased the author. He developed his plot quietly and showed in his drawing of Pip's weakness a greater subtlety in his understanding of character. He had intended a different ending from that we all know, which was substituted on the suggestion of Bulwer Lytton. It had seemed more natural to Charles for Pip finally to lose Estella, and many of his friends agreed with him. The happy ending was no particular favorite of his.

Through these years he was still giving readings all over the country and even in Paris, where his reception was beyond anything he had ever experienced. The French audience positively raised the roof with their applause which even followed him out to his carriage as he drove away from the hall.

He came to realize at length that reading and writing went ill together. He could do either, but not both. After *Great Expectations,* it was four years before he brought out another book.

They were years, too, of sad bereavement. His mother died, and so did Mrs. Hogarth, Henry Austin, and many friends, among them, Thackeray. His own son, Walter, died abroad. Then a winter of extra severity took a toll of his health. The thermometer was "I don't know where below freezing," he wrote to a friend. "The bath froze, and all the pipes froze and remained in a stony state for five or six weeks. The snow on the top of the house froze and was imperfectly removed with axes. My beard froze as I walked about, and I could not detach my cravat and coat from it until I was thawed at the fire. My boys and the officers stationed at Chatham skated away without a check to Gravesend—five miles off—and repeated the performance for three or four weeks."

He had much to see to outside as well as inside his house and after tramping about in heavy snow and being too impatient to change his boots, he got a touch of frostbite in his left leg, not recognized as such at the time. It gave him much pain and, though many remedies were tried, the leg troubled him all the rest of his life.

While he was planning the scene for Magwich's escape in *Great Expectations*, he had often wandered along the banks of the Thames, exploring riverside activities, and had noticed the many handbills pasted up on walls and fences giving descriptions of persons found drowned. They set him pondering on the means by which these bodies came ashore, and about the nature of the men whose living was earned so gruesomely. Out of these beginnings grew the story of *Our Mutual Friend*, and the characters of Hexam and Rogue Riderhood.

In the summer of 1865 he was caught in a railway accident as he returned from a visit to France. A bridge (at Staplehurst) collapsed as his train was passing over it, and he found his compartment hanging over a stream at a height of about fifteen feet above the water. He showed great presence of mind as he sought out the guard and obtained a key to unlock carriage doors and let people out. Then, seeing that many were badly hurt, he returned to his carriage for brandy and his hat to use as a basin. He went about giving aid to the injured until sufficient other help arrived. Some were so terribly mangled that he could hardly bear to look at them. More than one died as he raised their heads. The shock to his constitution was very great. The experience left its mark on him. Traveling suddenly became a misery and, even behind his own horses, he had sometimes to stop and get out when his nerves got the better of him.

Yet, eighteen months later he agreed to undertake a reading tour in America though it promised to be more exacting than anything he had ever done before.

His friends were horrified to find him contemplating such an expedition, but he was being pressed by various committees and syndicates on the other side of the Atlantic.

"They are bent upon my reading there, and they believe (on no foundation whatever) that I am going to read there," he wrote to Forster. "If I ever go, the time would be when the Christmas number goes to press. Early in this next November."

Weeks later he was still wavering. "You have no idea how heavily the anxiety of it sits upon my soul. But the prize looks so large."

With health he knew to be failing, financial security for the rest of his days seemed indeed a prize worth working for.

~~~~~~

CHAPTER XXII

"From These Garish Lights I Vanish Now for Ever More"

TWENTY-FOUR YEARS EARLIER THE MONTHLY INSTALL-
ments of *Martin Chuzzlewit* had been snatched from
the boat which had brought them from England and
publicly burned on the dock as a protest against
Charles' picture of American life. He still felt some
misgivings as to whether some old resentment might
not raise its head at sight of him, but the moment he
set foot on American soil he was reassured. As before,
he was met by cheering crowds, but the tone of their
greeting had changed. Mere curiosity had given way
to a deep sense of admiration, and of affection, too.
He was hailed as a master, venerated as one of the
immortals.

The tour was a triumph, successful "beyond description or exaggeration." No hall was large enough
to accommodate all who wanted to hear him. People
stood in line all day, thousands strong, in bitter weather
for tickets. In the streets speculators offered twenty
dollars down to anyone who would sell, knowing they
could get twice that amount for them. Perhaps the
record price was "fifty dollars and a brandy cock-
tail" for one ticket!

Charles found, to his cost, that his itinerary had

been badly planned by his agent, involving far too much traveling. He was always coming back to New York, and having to set out again to distant places. It was not long before the strain told on him. He suffered from severe catarrh. His heart was tired. He could not sleep. Letters home told of the triumph, but with none of his old fire. He got through the heavy programs only by fierce efforts of will and sheer dogged endurance. In town after town as the readings ended, crowds followed his carriage crying, "When will you come back?"—and could not believe him when he shook his head and replied sadly, "Never."

He understood very well the strain he was subjecting himself to and did not underestimate the seriousness of his symptoms.

The tour lasted five months and yielded, after all expenses had been met, the "prize" of one hundred thousand dollars. He had security indeed, but at what a cost!

Saying farewell at a public banquet in New York he spoke of the changes he had observed on this visit, of the rise of the cities, the increase in the amenities of life, the improvement in the tone of the press. He promised that, when he got back to England, he would write a postscript testifying to these changes, and would see that it appeared in all future editions of *Martin Chuzzlewit* and *American Notes*.

The voyage home, at the end of April, 1868, allowed him to rest. He so far recovered that, when they met him at Liverpool, his friends almost thought they must have been mistaken in their forebodings. His color was healthier, his eye clearer than they had expected. He had a great welcome home. At Gadshill, the houses along the road from the station were dressed with flags. The farmers from all around drove in in their chaises and cried, "Welcome Home, Sir!" as he drove between them in the old basket phaeton with Newman Noggs drawing it, and the two Newfoundland dogs running behind.

"The place is lovely and in perfect order," he wrote back to one of his American hostesses. "Birds sing all day and the nightingales all night."

According to Charles, when his doctor first saw him, he recoiled crying, "Good lord! Seven years younger!" And, thus encouraged, Charles set about arranging a farewell course of readings throughout the country.

Plorn, the youngest of his children, went out into the world that autumn. He was a dear, pleasant fellow, but without the least desire to fend for himself in any way. He had never done well at school, was happiest at home and preferred, of all things, to be out of doors. His father thought, therefore, that it might be a good plan for him to join his brother Alfred who was already in Australia. Plorn departed sadly. Indeed when the moment came for him to go, he and his father sat together on a station bench, silent, hands clasped, both in tears.

That was in September. Almost immediately afterwards, Henry, youngest but one, went up to Cambridge with a scholarship at Trinity Hall. Few things so pleased Charles—"But observe," he wrote to him, "we must have no shadow of debt. Square up everything—let not a farthing be outstanding on any account when we begin your allowance." He did not live to see it, but Henry did well at the University and (which would surely have given his father peculiar satisfaction) had a long and honorable career at the Bar, in the Courts where the abuses which Charles had exposed had all been done away with.

Charles had no intention of giving up and playing the invalid, though he was aware that his condition had not improved and did not yield to rest as he had hoped. He found himself "as sleepless as sick." Yet he went on with plans for more readings and even prepared a new one of the murder of Nancy from *Oliver Twist*. He confessed that it made his own hair rise on his head with horror, and set his pulses racing alarmingly, yet he was determined to give it to the public.

This reading fell into three parts, the first where Fagin set Noah Claypole to watch Nancy, the second on London Bridge, and the third, when Fagin made Claypole repeat his story to Sikes, so setting in train the fury of madness which led to Nancy's murder and his death.

A good deal of uneasiness was felt as to the effect of this reading on the public. Doctors warned Charles gravely that "if only one woman cries out when you murder the girl, there will be a contagion of hysteria all over the place."

He did not really believe them and decided to try it privately on a picked audience in London. "I want to leave behind me the recollection of something very passionate and dramatic," he insisted in reply to Forster's urgent remonstrance.

The trial performance was duly given and there was no panic, though certainly the drama was keenly felt. Macready came up from the country for it, and was full of praise and admiration. Charles had won his point, and proceeded to tour the country giving the new reading as often as four times a week until, at Preston

in April, he collapsed and his doctor forbade him ever
to read in public again.

Before going on to the platform that last evening,
he had remarked to a friend, "Don't say anything about
it, but the tremendously severe nature of this work is
a little shaking me. I feel extremely giddy, extremely
uncertain of my sense of touch both in my left leg
(which was the frostbitten one) and my left hand
and arm."

He gave one more reading, however, in London by
special request, but the effect on him was too desperate for even Charles to want to repeat it. On the
15th of March, 1870 he read for the last time and, said
Forster, had never read so well. He had chosen *A
Christmas Carol* and *Scenes from Pickwick*, and the
effect on him was terrible to behold. After he had
recovered his breath, he came back to the audience, a
drooping figure, to take his leave of them, saying:
"From these garish lights I vanish now for evermore
with a heartfelt, grateful, respectful and affectionate
farewell."

The previous evening he had begun a new story,
another tale of Rochester, *The Mystery of Edwin Drood,*
but the old spirit had gone out of him.

Some years earlier he had written to Forster, "It is
too late to say put the curb on, don't rush at hills—
and I am the wrong man to say it to. I have no relief
but in action. I am incapable of rest. I am confident
I should rust, break, die, if I spared myself. Much
better to die doing. . . . I have always felt of myself
that I must, please God, die in harness."

He died in harness, on the 9th of June, 1870.

He had spent that morning in the upper room of

the chalet, looking out on the freshness of a June morning and writing the sixth part of *Drood*.

Almost the last words he wrote were, "A brilliant morning shines on the old city. Its antiquities and ruins are surprisingly beautiful, with lusty ivy gleaming in the sun, and the rich trees waving in the balmy air. Changes of glorious light from moving boughs, songs of birds, scenes from gardens, woods, fields . . . penetrated into the Cathedral." From where he sat he could see those woods and fields, almost to the Cathedral.

He had been in good spirits that morning, and had said at breakfast that he thought he would write all day and not go for his usual walk or drive until the evening. At lunchtime he came back to the house and smoked a cigar in the conservatory. Mamey had gone to town for a few days and he and Georgina were alone. He went back to work cheerfully, returning an hour before dinner, very tired, silent and preoccupied. Even then he did not rest, but went to the library to attend to his letters.

Georgina was struck by his looks as they sat down to dinner and inquired in some alarm if he were feeling all right.

"Very ill," he replied, "I have been very ill this last hour."

He made an effort to go on with the meal, but it was clear he was suffering. Georgina begged him to go and lie down.

He replied very distinctly, "Yes, on the ground," and slid to the floor. In twenty-four hours he was dead.

He was buried in Westminster Abbey. His body

lies under the pavement in the Poets' Corner, with Thomas Hardy and Rudyard Kipling at his side.

The funeral was private and very quiet but the grave was kept open for two days, during which a constant stream of mourners came to stand beside it.

He was so widely beloved that, as the news became known, shabby people in mean streets and little shops, cabbies on their stands, turned to one another and said, "We have lost our friend."